:60 SECOND STRESS MANAGEMENT

:60 SECOND STRESS MANAGEMENT

Dr. Andrew Goliszek

New Horizon Press
Far Hills, New Jersey

New Horizon Press
P.O. Box 669
Far Hills, NJ 07931

Cover design: Norma Rahn
Interior design: Susan M. Sanderson

Library of Congress Catalog Card Number: 2003114431

Dr. Andrew Goliszek
  :60 Second Stress Management

ISBN: 0-88282-248-9
New Horizon Press

Manufactured in the U.S.A.

2008   2007   2006   2005   2004   /   5   4   3   2   1

To my wife, Kathy,
And our children,
Jennifer, David and Paul.
Their love, patience and support
helped me through the many
long hours it took
to complete this book.

Contents

Introduction ....*ix*

PART I: STRESS COPING AND :60 SECOND MANAGEMENTS
1. Stress: What It Is and What It Does 3
2. Signs, Symptoms and :60 Second Solutions 7
3. Good vs. Bad Stress 25
4. Job Stress and Burnout 33
5. Time Management 49
6. Stress and Mental Health 59
7. Childhood and Adolescent Stress 77
8. Stress and Aging 107

PART II: RELAXATION TECHNIQUES AND EXERCISES
9. Progressive Muscle Relaxation (PMR) 131
10. Tension/Relaxation 141
11. Meditation 147
12. Imaging Techniques and Self-healing.......................151
13. Nutrition and Stress..161
14. The Mind-Body Connection 169

PART III: SELF-HELP STRESS TESTS AND EVALUATIONS
15. Testing Your Stress Knowledge 185

Appendix 205

Introduction

Abraham Lincoln, whose responsibility and optimism in the darkest days of our country's history are unparalleled, once wrote:

"I am now the most miserable man living. If what I feel were equally distributed to the whole human family, there would be not one cheerful face on earth . . . I must die or be better."

The stress must have been getting to him.

It's been called the "disease of the twenty-first century," and it's believed to cause more illnesses than anything else known to modern medicine. And, whether we realize it or not, for most of us, it has become a habit we just can't seem to kick.

For years, doctors have warned us that stress is harmful to our health; they long ago discovered that being exposed to it on a regular basis can trigger major health problems such as cancer, hypertension and coronary heart disease. The latest evidence even indicates that it could be a major factor in the jump from HIV infection to active AIDS.

So, with all the bad news about stress, why has it been so hard for us to break the stress habit and just learn to relax? The answer may be that we don't treat our stress responses with the same respect we treat any other bad habit. In this fast-paced world, stress has become something we accept as a simple fact of life. We have learned to live—and die—with it. Changing our ingrained behavior takes time, but it can be done.

For many of us, stress has taken on a whole new meaning in the twenty-first century. Directly or indirectly, September 11, 2001 changed everything. From personal matters like the way we view the world around us and the manner in which we interact with our families to fiscal concerns like the probability of getting or keeping a job, the attitudes we have toward life and work in general have changed drastically. What we once considered important now may not seem as significant and the things we always took for granted probably carry a bit more weight.

Although time has a way of dampening the stress and trauma of that particular September day, we have found ourselves suddenly faced with an entirely new set of issues. Terrorism, unemployment, increasing violence, health scares like AIDS and SARS and destructive computer viruses are only a few of the problems we'll most likely have to cope with for some time to come. Sadly, in today's world, they're more likely to increase in frequency than fade away. And the more frequently we encounter these problems and the more we worry about how we'll be able to deal with them, the more conditioned we become to what we ultimately accept as "everyday stress." As it becomes a part of our lives, it becomes easier and easier to develop stress-related illnesses.

So how can you, as an individual, go about breaking your stress habit in order to raise your own quality of life? First, you can learn more about what stress is. Second, you can learn to recognize your own stress symptoms. Third, you can make changes in your ingrained behavior patterns to avoid stressors. And finally, by utilizing a series of quick and simple stress management relaxation techniques and exercises—:60 second stress managements—you can eliminate your own stress problems.

":60 second stress management" means simply that. Whatever relaxation techniques you employ, there's a window of opportunity in which to practice them: one short minute. The decision to act during that first minute of stress is critical. You must condition yourself to become a ":60 second stress manager."

Utilizing the techniques in this book, you'll soon discover that while life may have no shortage of stresses, proper stress management can become a normal and important part of your daily life. Realizing a calm, relaxed, stress-free feeling is easier than you might think. It's never more than sixty seconds away.

:60 SECOND STRESS MANAGEMENT

· PART I ·

STRESS COPING AND :60 SECOND MANAGEMENTS

· Chapter 1 ·

Stress: What It Is and What It Does

Harry comes home tired from a long day's work, still thinking about what tasks he didn't complete. When he tries to have have sex with his wife, he's still thinking about work and what he has to do the next day. Suddenly, he notices that he either cannot get an erection or cannot maintain one. Without realizing it, he blames his failure completely on himself. The next evening, he thinks about whether he will fail again. He tries harder and, because of his anxiety, fails again. The harder he tries, the more he fails. Soon, Harry begins to avoid intimacy and sexual contact altogether.

Harry is the victim of his own stress.

Stress isn't always such a bad thing. In fact, our ancestors depended upon natural stress responses for life itself—it was necessary to flee from predators, to fight enemies and to survive in a hostile world. Those who were successful in responding to life-threatening events survived; those who couldn't disappeared. Somewhere along the line, thanks to the marvelous process of evolution, we developed into "super responders." We became able to react immediately to almost any situation, yet found ourselves unable to control the world around us and the ways in which we reacted. As a result of this uncertainty, stress wove its way into every aspect of our society and became a part of our lives that we took for granted.

We respond to stress automatically, largely out of habit, to thousands of events in our lives. In today's world, stress stems less often from life-threatening situations. We have new concerns: our stress might be the result of having to deal with a high-tech career, a fast-paced business transaction, divorce, or social and family problems.

What began eons ago as a vital defense mechanism is today the leading cause of disease and illness in the modern world.

3

THE STRESS RESPONSE

You walk into your office Monday morning and see a stack of work. Something happens inside of you—you can sense it. If you're an over responder, your body may react with pain, nausea or anxiety. If you're a slow reactor, you may not get the message until you get home that evening or after you've gone to bed.

But, over responder or slow reactor, exactly the same things happen inside your body. No matter the source of stress or the time of reaction, the results are always the same. The person pressured by deadlines, the recent widow, the unprepared student or the patient who discovers he has a serious illness all experience different stressors, yet all respond in the same biological manner. Our stress responses have become so all-encompassing that we don't have to worry about what to respond to and what to ignore; we respond to everything.

STRESS RESPONSE AS A HABIT

A very common example of a stress-related response habit is male secondary impotence. Stress plays a major role in sexual problems because sexual activity is under the influence of the involuntary nervous system. Whenever a man gets aroused, nerve impulses from his brain cause blood vessels in the penis to dilate, allowing a flow of blood to enter the spongy tissue. At the same time, a sphincter muscle contracts and prevents blood from flowing back.

During any time of stress, in an unwelcome response, this sphincter muscle fails to contract and causes the penis to lose the blood needed for erection.

Here's a specific example:

John gets a new job and soon becomes irritated at some of the things his boss says to him. Since he needs the job, he can't do anything about it for fear of being fired. Every time he has a confrontation with his boss, John has a stress reaction. The reactions begin to come more and more easily, more quickly and are of longer duration with each experience. Eventually, the mere anticipation of his daily confrontations will bring about a stress reaction. He experiences negative reactions at home and on weekends, just by thinking about his boss. John's stress reaction has become a habit and gets progressively worse, more and more ingrained and harder to break.

From the moment we're born, we become creatures of habit. We use our habits to free our mind from routine tasks and to simplify our day-too-day existence. Habits are important. Simple tasks like writing, tying our shoes and eating with utensils are the direct result of habits. The problem occurs when we begin to acquire habits regardless of whether they're good or bad, positively or negatively reinforced.

Chronic stress response, then, is simply a bad habit that needs to be controlled. Our method of control will be a series of :60 second stress managements.

STRESS-RELATED
ILLNESSES AND DISEASES

A few of the diseases believed to be partly caused by long-term exposure to stress includes coronary heart disease, hypertension, kidney disease and arteriosclerosis. During the last decade, chronic backache, gastritis, migraine headaches, cold sores, hives and, most famously, ulcers also have been linked to chronic stress responses. The stress itself does not cause the illness but helps to bring it about by decreasing our immunological defenses.

Once we can discover the source of the stress and control it with a :60 second stress management technique, minor illnesses usually disappear.

How do we know that it is stress causing many of our problems?

In many parts of the world, where stress isn't a normal part of life, coronary heart disease is very rare. Once people in these areas are exposed to the stresses of modern society, studies show that they become as susceptible as anyone else to the stress-correlative diseases mentioned above. Other studies have shown that heart disease is linked to cholesterol levels, which increase with stress. We already know that smoking, obesity, alcohol consumption, kidney disorders, high salt intake and heredity can raise blood pressure; but now we also know that stress can be a major factor in triggering the onset of hypertension.

In one study of nine- to sixteen-year-olds, it was discovered that a routine act (albeit one that elicits a severe stress response in many people) such as reading out loud in front of classmates caused significant elevations in blood pressure. Studies continue to show that it's not only adults, but also children, who fall victim to hypertension as a direct result of stressful events in their lives.

Skin problems such as eczema, psoriasis and shingles have been treated by using stress management techniques, since many skin diseases have been linked to emotional stress.

Until recently, most illnesses were attributed to easily defined causes like diet, heredity, environment and lifestyle. Evidence now points in a new direction and links stress to a wide range of illnesses from headaches and ulcers to multiple sclerosis and cancer. Many of these illnesses and diseases can be controlled by learning to change attitudes and control thought patterns through simple :60 second management processes, which can help keep our immune systems from working overtime.

Managing stress is, without a doubt, one of the single most important elements in ensuring that your immunological defense is there and ready when it is needed the most. Studies show that stress can present problems beyond pesky headaches or a sleepless night spent worrying about the week's workload. It's vitally important in this increasingly stressed-out world that we train our bodies to respond positively to ever-present stressors. In doing so, we may be able to not only avoid disease and unrest, but allow ourselves to increase our level of happiness.

Throughout the rest of this book, we will attempt to isolate particular stress problems and alleviate them with specific :60 second stress managements. By conditioning yourself to spontaneously relax, to relieve tension, to cope with conflict and to eliminate anxiety, you'll gain freedom from stress and improve both the quantity and the quality of your life.

Chapter 2

Stress Signs, Symptoms and :60 Second Solutions

Bill starts having stomach pains when he goes to work. Instead of linking them to the stresses of his job, he looks to his diet, assuming that he's eating something that makes him ill. By automatically assuming that his stomach pain is caused by food, Bill ignores his body's cry for stress relief.

Joan begins to have back and neck pains during different parts of the day. She immediately assumes that the pains are being caused by the way she has been sleeping at night.

Both Bill and Joan are typical victims of stress without knowing it. They have not conditioned themselves to be aware of their bodies' stress signals.

The first step in relieving stress is to recognize certain easily definable symptoms that function as alarm bells to alert us that our body is being stressed. Regardless of how stress affects us individually, it always creates an unmistakable pattern of stress > symptom > illness. The trick in mastering our stress response is the ability to recognize the symptom quickly and link it to the stress reaction that it preceded. Further, recognizing certain stress-producing traits in our personality can help us to utilize our :60 second stress managements to relieve stress symptoms quickly and efficiently.

RECOGNIZING STRESS SYMPTOMS

Not every reaction we have is a symptom of stress; we're all different. What may be a stress signal for one individual may be a sign of disease for another. Stress symptoms can be divided into three categories: physical, emotional and behavioral. Many of the symptoms listed below start out as minor irritants, but become progressively worse and may lead to serious stress-related diseases.

Physical Symptoms

- headaches
- twitching eyelid
- twitching nose
- facial or jaw pains
- dry mouth or throat
- difficulty in swallowing
- ulcers on tongue
- neck pains
- dizziness
- speech difficulties, slurring, or stuttering
- backaches
- muscle aches
- weakness
- constipation
- indigestion
- nausea and/or vomiting
- diarrhea
- gain or loss of weight
- loss of appetite or constant appetite

- rashes, hives or other skin problems

- chest pains

- heartburn

- heart palpitations

- frequent urination

- cold hands and/or feet

- excessive sweating

- insomnia

- excessive sleeping

- sexual inadequacy

- high blood pressure

- chronic fatigue

- swollen joints

- increased allergies

- frequent colds and flu

- trembling and/or nervous tics

- accident proneness

- excessive menstruation or menstrual distress

- rapid or difficult breathing

Emotional Symptoms

- irritability

- moodiness

- depression

- unusual aggressiveness

- loss of memory or concentration

- restlessness or over excitability

- nervousness about little things

- nightmares

- impulsive behavior

- feelings of helplessness or frustration

- withdrawal from other people

- neurotic behavior

- racing thoughts or disorientation

- anger

- inability to make decisions

- anxiety

- feelings of panic

- frequent episodes of crying

- thoughts of suicide

- feelings of losing control

- lack of sexual interest

- periods of confusion

Behavioral Symptoms

- gnashing or grinding teeth

- wrinkling forehead

- high-pitched nervous laughter

- foot or finger tapping

- nail biting

- hair pulling or twirling

- increased smoking

- increased use of prescribed medication

- increased alcohol consumption

- compulsive dieting

- binge eating

- pacing the floor

- chronic procrastination

- loss of interest in physical appearance

- sudden change in social habits

- chronic tardiness

One reason we don't recognize minor stress symptoms is that we've become used to looking for the more common physical signals. Almost any kind of symptom can be a hidden signal of stress. By learning to recognize the small, insignificant signals, we can become more aware of our own sources of stress, and prevent ourselves from developing more serious symptoms. This ability will make it far easier to manage our stress reactions.

LINKING STRESS
SYMPTOMS TO
STRESS SOURCES

One of the best ways to identify stress response patterns or hidden sources of stress is to keep a stress diary for at least two or three weeks.

The following is a sample of what your diary might look like—divided into four columns: Time of Day, Stress Symptom, Immediate Activity and Previous Activity.

As soon as we notice a stress symptom we should write it down immediately, along with the time of day it occurs, the activity at the time and the thoughts we were having, and the activities and thoughts prior to the stress symptom. It is very important to include our thoughts as well as our physical activities, because thoughts can be just as potent as actions.

It is just as important to include previous activities and thoughts. Stress reactions do not always occur at the same time that stress occurs. To get a true indication, we need to train ourselves to look back and remember what we have experienced during the past several hours.

After a week of keeping a stress diary, it is time to start looking for

Time of Day	Stress Symptom	Immediate Activity	Previous Activity
9:30 A.M.	Headache	Having break-fast alone	Rushing to get kids to school
12:30 P.M.	Muscle pain in shoulders, neck	Watching T.V.	Thinking about paying bills
6:00 P.M.	Tapping foot constantly	Thinking about unpaid bills	Thinking about unpaid bills
10:00 P.M.	Stomach pain	Argument with daughter	Watching T.V.
12:00 P.M.	Insomnia	Feeling anger about argument	Feeling anger about argument

patterns. Do you usually get symptoms at a certain time of day? Do you get a specific symptom every time you do a certain task or think a certain thought? Do you get sick an hour or more after you do something?

This is when we can play detective and look for the clues that will lead us to our own hidden sources of stress. For example, we may notice that at 9:30 A.M. almost every day, we get a terrible headache. On closer inspection, we see that at 9:00 A.M. each day, we were busy rushing the kids off to school. On Monday, Tuesday and Friday, we had trouble falling asleep. Our diary tells us that on those nights, we thought a lot about problems at work. At 7:00 P.M. on Wednesday and Thursday, we had diarrhea. According to our stress diary, at 5:30 P.M. on those nights, we were worried about having to go to weekly staff meetings while leaving the kids at home alone.

Once we recognize our stress symptoms and link them to their stress sources, the next step is to determine why the sources are causing the symptoms. We should ask ourselves four questions:

1. Is the timing of the activity (time of day or night) causing stress symptoms?

2. Is the reason we're doing the activity causing stress symptoms?

3. Is the way we're doing the activity causing stress symptoms?

4, Is the amount of time spent doing the activity causing stress symptoms?

First, we need to assess whether or not it's the timing of whatever we're doing that's creating problems. Do the symptoms disappear when we change the time of activity? Could nighttime be better than daytime? Would reorganizing our schedule make what we're doing less stressful? Next, we need to assess why we're doing what we're doing in the first place. Is it really necessary? Can we do without it? Then, we need to assess the manner in which we're doing what we're doing. Are we too intense? Do we worry the entire time? Do we use so much energy that having completed the task, we feel worn out? Finally, we need to assess how much time we spend doing what we're doing. Do we spend too much time on the activity? Do we have too little time to accomplish the task? Is the amount of time we spend interfering with other, more important things?

The answers to these questions can tell us why the things we do or the feelings we have make us stressed and sick. Keeping an accurate stress diary will offer you physical proof that some of the little things we do and the little thoughts we think may not be so little after all! Your diary will provide the evidence you need to start making informed decisions about your body and changes to your stressful patterns.

At the end of each week of our stress diary, we need to write down three things: the exact causes of our various stress symptoms, be it a physical activity, a thought, etcetera, the reason why the activity is causing the symptoms, whether it is the timing or the reason or the way we undertake the activity and finally, our goals for eliminating the stress symptoms. For example, we could write something like this:

1. Cause of headaches: rushing to get the kids off to school every morning.

2. Reasons for symptoms: timing—not enough time to do everything—I feel rushed.

3. Solutions: a) get up a little earlier
                b) organize my morning hours more efficiently
                c) don't leave things till the last minute
                d) prepare the night before

After formulating a plan to confront our stressors, we should check our stress diary each day so we're sure of meeting our goals. As we accomplish one goal, we need to move on to the next until we eliminate stress symptoms altogether. Eventually, our natural ability to recognize stress symptoms will become increasingly fine-tuned. We'll be able to identify stress sources instantly and act quickly to mediate them before they trigger a conditioned stress response.

Even certain personality traits can be adjusted for our benefit if we recognize those traits as sources of stress. Type A individuals, for example, are more prone to stress symptoms and stress reactions because they often don't link their symptoms with their normal behavior patterns. For them, keeping a stress diary is even more important than it is for the rest of use. But regardless of what personality type we are, we all need to realize that small and insignificant events can be major sources of stress and illness.

RECOGNIZING TYPE A VS. TYPE B BEHAVIOR

When heart disease became our nation's number one killer, it was thought that anyone leading a stressful lifestyle was at risk. It's now well known that there's a certain behavior pattern called "Type A," which makes those that exhibit these characteristics more susceptible to coronary heart disease and other stress-related diseases because of specific character traits and mental attitudes. Sometimes, these traits and attitudes are the reason for stress symptoms in the first place. Modifying Type-A behavior patterns in order to relieve stress symptoms requires that we identify the traits in ourselves that make us either Type A or Type B individuals. We can then use stress management techniques to gradually condition ourselves to alter those traits.

Following are some differences between Type A individuals and Type B individuals. Not all Type As and Type Bs will have all or even most of these traits, but people typically fall into one or the other category.

Type A Characteristics

- Intensely competitive

- Impatient

- Achievement oriented

- Aggressive and driven

- Having a distorted sense of time urgency

- Moving rapidly and frequently

- Talking fast and listening impatiently

Type B Characteristics

- Relaxed and unhurried

- Patient

- Noncompetitive

- Nonaggressive

- Not having baseless time urgency issues

In addition to these basic character traits, Type A individuals have been proven to have a greater cardiovascular response to stress, higher blood pressure, a greater release of adrenaline during times of stress, higher blood cholesterol levels and more extensive arteriosclerosis than Type B individuals. Type A individuals generally don't have all these problems at the same time or even as a general rule, but normally they have enough of them to increase their chances of becoming sick with stress-related diseases earlier in life than Type B individuals.

BEHAVIOR TYPE QUIZ

Many times, stress symptoms are the direct result of Type A behavior. Unless we become aware of our own Type A traits, recognizing stress symptoms and linking them to stress sources can be very difficult. The following quiz is designed to give you an idea of your own behavioral type. Read each statement carefully and then circle the number corresponding to the category of behavior that best fits you. (1 = Never; 2 = Seldom; 3 = Sometimes; 4 = Usually; 5 = Always). When you finish, add up all the circled numbers. A key at the end of the quiz will explain what your total score means.

1. I become angry or irritated   1   2   3   4   5
   whenever I have to stand in
   line for more than 15 minutes.

2. I handle more than one   1   2   3   4   5
   problem at a time.

3. It's hard finding the time to   1   2   3   4   5
   relax and let myself go during
   the day.

4. I become irritated or annoyed   1   2   3   4   5
   when some is speaking too
   slowly.

5. I try hard to win at sports   1   2   3   4   5
   or games.

6 When I lose at sports or games,   1   2   3   4   5
   I get angry at myself or others.

7. I have trouble doing special   1   2   3   4   5
   things for myself.

8. I work much better under pressure or when meeting deadlines.

    1   2   3   4   5

9. I find myself looking at my watch whenever I'm sitting around or not doing something active.

    1   2   3   4   5

10. I bring work home with me.

    1   2   3   4   5

11. I feel energized and exhilarated after being in a pressure situation.

    1   2   3   4   5

12. I feel like I need to take charge of a group in order to get things moving.

    1   2   3   4   5

13. I find myself eating rapidly in order to get back to work.

    1   2   3   4   5

14. I do things quickly regardless of whether I have time or not.

    1   2   3   4   5

15. I interrupt what people are saying when I think they're wrong.

    1   2   3   4   5

16. I'm inflexible and rigid when it comes to changes at work or at home.

    1   2   3   4   5

17. I become jittery and need to move whenever I'm trying to relax.

    1   2   3   4   5

18. I find myself eating faster than the people I'm eating with.

    1   2   3   4   5

19. At work, I need to perform more than one task at a time in order

    1   2   3   4   5

to feel productive.

20. I take less vacation time than   1   2   3   4   5
    I'm entitled to.

21. I find myself being very picky   1   2   3   4   5
    and looking at small details.

22. I become annoyed at people   1   2   3   4   5
    who don't work as hard as I do.

23. I find that there aren't enough   1   2   3   4   5
    things to do during the day.

24. I spend a good deal of my time
    thinking about my work.   1   2   3   4   5

25. I get bored very easily.   1   2   3   4   5

26. I'm active on weekends either   1   2   3   4   5
    working or doing projects.

27. I get into arguments with people   1   2   3   4   5
    who don't think my way.

28. I have trouble "rolling with   1   2   3   4   5
    the punches" whenever
    problems arise.

29. I interrupt someone's conversation 1   2   3   4   5
    in order to speed things up.

30. I take everything I do seriously.   1   2   3   4   5

The minimum score is 30, the maximum 150. The breakdown by personality type is as follows:

SCORE   **PERSONALITY TYPE**
100-150   Type A
76-99   Type AB (Average)
30-75   Type B

If your score was 75 or below, you're a Type B person. You pretty much take life as it comes and usually don't allow problems and worries to dominate your life. If your score was in the range of 76 to 99, you're part of a majority who has some Type A and some Type B characteristics. For the most part, you know how to relax and aren't very aggressive or competitive. You do, however, take some things seriously and, in certain situations, like to be active, competitive and productive. You need to see which Type A traits you have and decide whether or not they're affecting your health and lifestyle. If your score was 100 or above, then chances are you're a Type A person and, while you're a go-getter and display many characteristics of driven, successful people, you may need to work on certain attitudes, behaviors and priorities that put you at greater risk of stress-related illnesses.

Because every person is different, there are no absolute right or wrong answers to the test, and not every person scored as a Type A or Type B exhibits all of the respective behaviors or is exposed to the same health risks. For example, a traumatic experience for one person may be a cakewalk for someone else, regardless of their personality type. But no one, regardless of how energized and excited stress makes them feel, can keep up with too many Type A behavior patterns and stay healthy for very long. In fact, it's well known that Type A personalities suffer from many more symptoms of stress and get sick more frequently than Type B personalities do.

Type B or Type AB behavior is good because it allows us to achieve goals, to be motivated and productive and to do all the things Type A personalities can do without being hostile, aggressive, impatient or insecure. Achieving everything we want while still maintaining our composure and being able to relax is something we all can learn to do. By modifying our Type A behavior patterns and conditioning ourselves to adopt more Type B character traits, we'll become sick less often and make our lives more enjoyable and stress free.

MODIFYING TYPE A
CHARACTER TRAITS

We develop either Type A or Type B behavior as a result of our upbringing, our environment and sometimes our genetic makeup. Therefore, modifying Type A behavior patterns in order to develop more Type B behavior patterns can't be achieved overnight. It takes practice, effort and a sincere desire for change. Once we begin the process of adopting more Type B traits, however, it becomes easier and easier to adjust our behaviors because our brain will be trained to look at stressful situations in new and different ways.

The key to modifying Type A behavior is to break some of the long-term stress habits we've acquired. We do this by practicing special exercises that force us to replace our old habits with newer, healthier ones. Many of us have Type A traits not because we're born with them, but because we've repeated Type A behavior patterns so often they've become an unnatural part of our real personality. Moreover, in many instances, society rewards Type A behavior. In essence, we teach ourselves some of the bad Type A habits. By actually practicing Type B behavior exercises, we can gradually condition ourselves to eliminate some of the most harmful and most obvious Type A behavior traits. Once that happens, we will be able to confront stressful situations with the knowledge that we can use our new Type B habits to combat stress and prevent its symptoms.

OVERCOMING STRESS-RELATED TYPE A ANGER

Anger is the trait most responsible for the negative health effects of Type A behavior. The inability to control anger can lead to premature heart attacks or other illnesses. Anger, be it either the result of stress or a cause, hinders our ability to function effectively and maintain a well-balanced and healthy life.

As we grow up, we learn to use our anger in many different ways and to see the many varieties of anger response and use. Just look around. Some people use it to get attention, others to get what they want and still others to vent feelings of frustration or aggression. In the past, experts have assured us that it was better to release anger than to keep it contained, but, as more studies have been done, it has become clearer that the most effective and healthy way to deal with anger is to prevent it from occurring at all or, if that is not possible, to direct it into a more appropriate channel.

:60 SECOND STRESS MANAGEMENTS FOR ANGER

1. *Learn to be assertive.* Begin slowly if you feel uncomfortable. Try to take just one minute a day to look for opportunities to communicate confidently about minor issues. You can build up confidence to express feelings spontaneously and non-aggressively. (Making a list of these is helpful.)

2. *Identify the source of your anger.* Whenever you become angry, take sixty seconds to make sure you focus your emotion on the

specific reason for that anger. Once you channel your anger appropriately, it will become easier to work on strategies that will eliminate the source of frustration.

3. *Use a third party to intervene.* Direct communication is not always possible. Take a minute to find and utilize a third party as a sounding board rather than, in the heat of the moment, cause a destructive conflict. Try to resolve anger-causing conflicts as quickly as possible by working through someone you feel is willing, qualified and able to assist.

4. *Try to be more understanding.* Try to become more aware of what the person with whom you are angry may feel. By nature, when we become more sympathetic to others, we have a tendency to become less aggressive and more accommodating. Take sixty seconds to define and consider the feelings of others and recognize how those feelings may create even more anger for both of you.

5. *Find ways to prevent anger-causing situations.* Anger situations are often recurring problems. Identify the cause of your anger and find solutions to eliminate or bypass that cause. Anger can actually become intensified by repetition. Take sixty seconds to sit down with pencil and paper and diagram a method to eliminate the problem. This activity alone will relieve angry feelings because you will be reacting positively and constructively to your anger.

:60 SECOND TYPE B
BEHAVIOR EXERCISES

There are several practical exercises we can do to change our Type A habits and activities. After repeatedly completing these exercises, they will eventually become automatic :60 second stress managements and can even allow us to think up unique and personal managements by using our own particular Type A behavior patterns. Practicing these exercises regularly is important in habit formation because the physical act is a more powerful conditioner than just contemplation. Conditioning, whether physical or mental, requires both mental and physical effort to achieve positive lasting effects.

1. *Determine what activities arouse Type A behavior and reenact them utilizing Type B behavior.* Take sixty seconds to list them. For

instance, if standing in a line triggers stress symptoms, the next time you have to stand in a line consciously practice not being irritated or annoyed. Think about a pleasant upcoming weekend, a funny thing you read or saw on television or a favorite experience. Thinking about pleasant things will eventually come easily and naturally.

2. *While eating, put your utensils down between bites.* Count to twenty. This will force you to slow your eating pattern and leave more time for calming conversation and positive interaction. Slowing down your eating habits will spill over into other activities, helping you to slow them down as well.

3. *Force yourself to do more recreational activities.* Take sixty seconds to make a list of things you might enjoy. For instance, instead of reading job-related material, buy a book and enjoy it purely for the sake of reading. Make a date with yourself to go to a fun movie, take a joyous ride in the country or walk in the woods. In a short period of time, you can make yourself feel special and by omission, become more aware of any negative behavior patterns affecting your health.

4. *Spend an entire day without your watch.* Make a real effort to forget time. A few days without your watch will make you aware of how nice it is not to be a clock watcher.

5. *Pay attention to every frown and negative facial expression.* This exercise will train you to become acutely aware of the difference between negative and positive expressions. At the end of the day, take sixty seconds to write down what you noticed about your facial expressions. After a week or two, a negative facial expression will instantly trigger an awareness of a destructive action. Being aware of negative expressions also will allow you to instantly recognize sources of negative stress by noting what provoked your frown.

6. *Give yourself positive Type B self instructions.* Take sixty seconds to make a list of Type B self instructions. Don't be afraid to verbalize Type B expressions—relax, slow down, stay calm, don't rush, easy does it, etcetera—out loud. Actually hearing them will add to their effectiveness. Eventually, they will become so automatic that you'll be able to retrieve them from your subconscious without having to verbalize at all.

7. *Reward yourself.* Take ten seconds to choose a Type B behavior pattern. Follow it for an entire week. At the end of a successful

week of positive behavior, reward yourself with something special. Recognizing your accomplishment with a reward strengthens the conditioning process.

At the end of our stress diary, we should set a section aside for writing down our Type A character traits, our goals for modifying them into Type B character traits and whether or not any of our stress symptoms can be eliminated by changing from Type A to Type B behavior patterns. Here's how it might look:

Type A Traits	Type A Stress Symptoms	Goals for Modifying Type A Behavior	Symptoms Eliminated?
Impatient about waiting	1. Grinding teeth 2, Neck pains	Think postive thoughts when waiting in a line	1. Yes 2. Yes
Overscheduling work: trying to do too much	1. Headaches	Schedule only one thing at a time. Take periodic breaks.	1. Yes
Always in a rush to go somewhere	1. Stomach pains 2. General muscle tension	Get up earlier, do advance planning and organize time better	1. No 2. Yes

The idea behind practicing Type B character traits and keeping stress diary records is that once we recognize stress symptoms, become more aware of our behavior and repeatedly perform constructive activities to modify that behavior, Type A stress management becomes a spontaneous one-minute mental exercise. That is, we eventually teach ourselves to "turn off" Type A character traits and "turn on" Type B character traits in as little as one minute because our brain will be conditioned to guide our behavior in a Type B way. This doesn't come easily at first, since we've spent a lifetime acquiring Type A habits. But if we use the simple principle of habit formation by conscientiously undertaking Type B activities and responses, we can gradually eliminate almost any negative Type A habit. Having done so, we'll not only become healthier and happier, but we'll feel better about ourselves for having the strength to change our own negative habits.

· Chapter 3 ·

Good vs. Bad Stress

Recently, a group of lawyers were studied in relation to stress. It was discovered that the ones who became sick most often were the least stressed—exactly the opposite of what was expected! Confused examiners delved deeper into the study and found that the unexpected result was clarified when the manner in which lawyers were trained during law school was taken into consideration. For four years, they had been conditioned to believe that they performed better under pressure. When that pressure failed to materialize, they responded in the opposite way from the average person, who is most likely conditioned to respond negatively to stress.

Notwithstanding differences in source, the stress response is basically the same in each of us. The degree to which it affects us depends entirely on how we handle it. Viewing stress, as the lawyers in the study did, for its constructive possibilities, rather than as nothing more than a destructive cause of problems, is the first step to becoming a healthier, stress-free person.

STRESS TOLERANCE

We sometimes hear people say, "I work better under pressure" or "I thrive on competition." These are individuals who automatically perform better when they're under the gun. Seemingly more satisfied when they are meeting deadlines, rushing to make sales or doing anything that enhances the excitement of their lives, they are members of a minority for whom stress is not necessarily harmful and actually may be part and parcel of a healthy and productive life. For them, stress tolerance automatically takes negative situations and transforms them into positive events.

Our goal is to develop the kind of stress tolerance these people have without changing our personalities and without needing pressure to feel good about ourselves and our abilities. Learning to do this is one of the critical elements in stress management.

One of the most popular theories about stress suggests that stress-tolerant individuals possess an attitude of control, commitment and a sense of purpose in life. Stress-prone individuals, on the other hand, often feel powerless about the events surrounding them. In general, we can say that "good stress" results from situations we can control and "bad stress" results from situations over which we have no control.

Stress perception is influenced by many factors, including but not limited to age, intelligence, income, physical ability, level of education and religion. For example, if we are expected to solve a difficult problem, we are naturally less stressed if we have the education, intelligence and resources to solve a given problem. Likewise, if we are financially secure, the issue of job security is not nearly as stressful as it would be if we needed our job in order to support a family. In essence, the way we perceive stressors and the level of significance we ascribe to them is the critical factor in how we ultimately cope.

POSITIVE AND NEGATIVE PERCEPTIONS

The first—and most important—mental reaction that occurs when we encounter any kind of situation or event is our perception of that event as either positive or negative.

A study done with nurses showed that those not involved in intensive care units experienced much higher levels of anxiety, reported more physical ailments and had greater workload dissatisfaction than those who were involved in high-stress positions. The indication was that intensive care nurses wanted (or needed) a more challenging environment, and in general, felt more adventurous and capable of handling any situation that could arise.

This and other studies indicate that certain individuals respond to stress in a positive way, because they are able to perceive stressful sequences of events as challenging, rewarding experiences. This type of stress tolerance is achieved early in the developmental process and remains with us as a positive habit throughout life.

But even if we don't develop that tolerance, we still have control over how we respond to stress by using the power of our brain and our :60 second stress managements to change our perceptions. Once we utilize these techniques, we can overcome our own natural tendencies to be stress prone and join the ranks of the stress-tolerant.

STRESS TYPES

Relative to stress and lifestyle, there are more or less three types of individuals: the type who can't get along well without a stressful lifestyle, the type who can't get along well without a quiet, peaceful life and the type who has the ability to get along perfectly with or without stress. As demonstrated by our ancestral stress responses, a certain amount of stress is essential for normal health, so long as the amount doesn't exceed the coping ability of our own personality. The danger comes when we mismatch our personality type with an aggressive, high-stress lifestyle. When we exceed our tolerances, our normal personality becomes inhibited and we either get too much or too little stress.

Unfortunately, it can be very difficult to gauge our own stress tolerances, and many individuals in high-stress careers make the mistake of thinking that they as a group (e.g., lawyers or emergency room doctors) are stress-tolerant by virtue of their career path. Jobs don't make people stress-tolerant. If that were true, there wouldn't be so many heart attack and ulcer victims among executives, doctors and air traffic controllers. Individuals often adopt an overwhelming stress load without developing a proper attitude or without using stress-management techniques to help them boost their tolerance. Assuming that we're stress-tolerant is a deadly mistake, especially if we've been subconsciously conditioned to be prone to stress all along.

Knowing which personality type we are is important in deciding our occupations, choosing a lifestyle and acknowledging the kinds of activities we need to avoid. Before we can work toward becoming stress-tolerant, we need to examine the type of personality we have in order to accomplish the transition to stress tolerance in a healthy fashion.

Unfortunately, most of us don't have the luxury of choosing what our day-to-day experiences will be like. We go to work and are forced to confront situations that lead to stress, anxiety and depression. Some of us feel helpless and alienated, because we can't or won't take control over the events in our lives. These feelings intensify and can eventually morph into major emotional problems leading to ulcers, heart attacks, hypertension and many other stress-related illnesses. To prevent these unwelcome consequences, we need to develop a "stress-plus" or "stress-tolerant" attitude. This kind of attitude changes the way our brain interprets events and will condition us to automatically or habitually turn negative situations into positive experiences.

:60 SECOND STRESS
TOLERANT
MANAGEMENTS

Stress tolerance begins in the brain. It is there that we must attack and change our conditioning processes. During this stage, there are five mental images that must be present to help stress work for us instead of against us. The mental images must be repeated until they become part of our day-to-day existence, part of our unconscious behavior and firmly ingrained as habits. Once they become part of our normal thinking process, they will become automatic :60 second management switches, turning our stress to a natural and positive response.

Mental Image #1. *I get a feeling of accomplishment and strength whenever I'm committed or involved.*

Whenever we commit to a project, activity or job, we derive a sense of worth that's important in how we feel about ourselves and what we're doing with our lives. Becoming actively involved and committed gives us purpose and direction. We begin to lose negative attitudes brought on by stress. Most of us tend to be passive rather than active in many areas of our lives, but by actively participating in the world and being involved and committed, we can gain a better outlook on life and, in general, feel much better about ourselves. When that happens, we'll automatically begin to experience more positive and less negative events.

Mental Image #2. *I find change and/or challenge an exciting and rewarding experience.*

Too often we view changes in our lives as negative experiences. Even more often we allow changes to take control of our lives without making any effort at all to make positive experiences out of them. And sometimes we view change as neither positive nor negative and develop an attitude of complacency that causes us to have little if any feeling of excitement about anything and removes any semblance of control. We always should be prepared to visualize the positive aspects of change rather than dwell on the minus side. Get in the habit of thinking about any change or challenge as exciting and rewarding. The more you do this, the less negativity you'll feel and the more excited you'll be.

A simple trick to use whenever we find that a change in our routine causes anxiety is to do something special for ourselves at the start of each day. For example, we can begin the day by taking a leisurely walk, having a cup of tea and reading the paper or sitting quietly and listening to our favorite program on the radio. Going out of the way and taking a few minutes to do a little something extra for ourselves can make us feel special and give us the incentive to go out and meet those changes and challenges with a capable and positive attitude.

Mental Image #3. *I get a feeling of power that energizes me whenever I take control of situations.*

A sense of control over the events and situations in our daily lives is probably the most important and fundamental attitude we need in order to turn bad stress into good stress. We're discovering that bad stress isn't just a consequence of job pressures and negative events, but rather of feelings of uselessness and powerlessness within a big and incomprehensible world. There's absolutely no way that we can make any kind of positive use of a stressful situation unless we know that we can exert control over our experience. If we feel in control, we can easily channel our energy into constructive and rewarding activities.

One of the biggest problems we face as stress-prone individuals is an inability to maintain command over events of which we should have had control all along. The more we lose control or control is taken from us, the more negatively we begin to feel and the more stressed we become. Eventually, the problem compounds and every situation we encounter is one that we have little or no control over at all.

Experiencing control is actually directly related to our involvement and commitment to the world around us, because these give us a sense of control and allow us to develop behavior patterns that automatically put us in command of situations, thereby reducing stress. Once we begin to feel like we're in charge of situations, we start meeting them head-on, instead of worrying about how they'll affect us. Soon, we realize that *controlling* is much easier and more rewarding for us than always *being* controlled.

Mental Image #4. *Stress can bring out the qualities in me that make me most productive and worthwhile.*

Why would we want to think that anything has the power to make us worthless and unproductive? Why should we deny ourselves the opportunity to be a better person just because we happen to be under pressure or stress? Imagine stress to be a battery that energizes you, one without which you wouldn't be able to reach your full potential.

Good athletes know that in order to perform well, they need intense competition and pressure. The great ones have developed the attitude that unless they're under pressure, they're just not going to be at their peak. This is why most world sporting records are set during the Olympics or during competitions when the best athletes are competing. Most athletes, given lack of outside pressure, can only challenge themselves to do better than the last time. These individuals believe that only the stress of intense competition brings out their best qualities. Their bodies respond to what their brains have been conditioned to perceive and, therefore, they use that extra pressure to stimulate themselves into making stress work for them. We all need to become like athletes in the sense that our performances and attitudes always will be better when we're challenged. We'll quickly discover how effective stress can be in giving us the incentive to do our very best.

Mental Image #5. *I can transform any stressful situation into something positive.*

There's absolutely no reason why we can't think of something positive that will result from most stressful situations. When we put this idea into practice, we'll have overcome the biggest obstacle to becoming stress tolerant! The idea that we should be able to transform something negative into something positive is, in a way, a culmination of the first four mental images. If we become involved and committed, we'll begin to have a feeling of control over challenges and experience the ability to make those situations exciting and rewarding. Once that happens, we'll subconsciously and automatically believe that those same situations bring out the best in us and make us more productive and worthwhile. All these factors naturally will make us feel we can turn just about any negative event into a positive experience.

Integrating these mental images into our own personalities conditions us to make a conscientious effort to adopt a positive attitude about stress. The attitude we choose determines whether or not we allow events to control us or whether we control them and, consequently, whether or not we perceive stress as a challenge that we can overcome and mold to our own benefit. This small adjustment in the way we view challenges is the basic precept behind stress tolerance. By incorporating this simple principle into our daily lives, we can turn stress into a driving force that will enable us to perceive negative events in a very positive and constructive way.

:60 SECOND STRESS MANAGEMENTS FOR TURNING BAD STRESS INTO GOOD STRESS

Changing some of our behavior patterns is critical to :60 second stress management and in developing stress tolerance. There are several basic methods of changing attitudes that will quickly lead to :60 second stress management techniques.

1. *Engage in positive personal dialogue.* Whenever we find ourselves in stressful situations we should take a minute to find something positive in the event. The worst thing we can do is say something negative to ourselves.

2. *Visualize positive results.* It is common, when under stress, to visualize what we expect to happen. It's important to visualize a positive outcome. Stop and take :60 seconds to think about a good result. Expect success and you'll be that much closer to reaching a successful outcome.

3. *Be flexible enough to change.* We shouldn't hesitate to change the way we approach problems. By being flexible, we may find a better method of accomplishing our goals and organizing our lives. We should have the wisdom and courage to do things a new and better way.

4. *Take time out.* Few of us can work for more than three or four hours straight without losing our ability to concentrate. We need a break every few hours to set our minds free and get back into a good frame of mind. Take a minute to schedule time for lunch, dinner or entertainment. Taking time for ourselves makes us feel we are important and gives us a sense of self-worth. When we treat ourselves as special individuals, we automatically have a better outlook on life and improve our capacity to change our attitudes.

5. *Find the best work time and environment.* Most of us are either morning or night people. Determine your best time and plan your schedule, as much as possible, around that time and your peak energy levels.

6. *Exercise.* Exercise is one of the best ways to relieve tension and anxiety. It not only makes us feel energized and invigorated, but it also gives our immune system a boost. Moreover, exercise releases endorphins, which not only suppress pain but act to give us feelings of well-being and even euphoria.

7. *Don't dwell on the past.* We can't do anything about the past. We can only control the present and perhaps the future.

Instead of worrying about what has happened in the past, we should take a minute to use past experiences in a positive way: "Okay, I didn't want to do it that way. I'll do it this way next time." Then, forget about it and go on to more important things.

8. *Change or avoid the situation.* All of us have traits in our personalities that simply will not allow us to cope with certain situations, even if we change our attitudes and behavior. When this happens, change or avoid the situation entirely. This may be hard to do, especially if it involves job or career, but most people will find that using all the :60 second stress management techniques available will help them improve their situations to the point of being able to cope with the most adverse conditions.

Turning negative events into positive experiences requires that we make adjustments in the way we think and in the way we act. Regardless of the kinds of personality we have, conditioning ourselves to cope with stress by changing our attitudes and behavior is the key element in developing a stress-tolerant lifestyle.

Each of us falls into a certain personality mold that gives us character and makes us a unique individual with different interests and singular behavior patterns. Somewhere within all of us, however, lies the ability to bring out the best in ourselves. We have the power to turn bad stress into good. How we perceive life events, how we behave in response to stress encounters and how we condition ourselves to look at negative situations in a positive way determines how quickly and easily we can begin to break the stress habit.

· Chapter 4 ·

Job Stress and Burnout

Bob became a teacher with the hope of making a real impact on children's lives. He graduated with the high hopes and unshakable faith of an idealistic young man. By his third year of teaching, Bob had become frustrated by poor working conditions, an unsupportive administration, angry, critical parents and undisciplined students. The harsh realities began to take their toll. Bob lost his enthusiasm, developed negative feelings, came to classes unprepared and became detached from his students and fellow teachers. Eventually, the profession Bob once loved very much made him so ill that he chose to change careers.

The attitude that work is a duty and an obligation began in the earliest days of civilization, deeply rooted in religious and social mores that defined what was considered "good" values. Pilgrims brought these beliefs, tempered with an unshakable faith in the future, to America. They believed that success and survival could be achieved only through cooperation, determination, and hard labor. This positive attitude toward work continued for generations, until a new and totally different society began to evolve. We developed the notion that anything was possible if only we worked hard enough to accomplish our goals. And as our society has developed, so has our concept of work. Instead of asking, "How will my work affect my neighbors?" we have begun to ask, "How will I be affected by what I do?"

Gradually, work as a means of improving society was replaced by work as a means of enhancing our own status and standard of living. With the birth of the "me" generation, work has become yet another source of stress. As job stress becomes such a routine part of our daily lives, relieving stress through changes in our work habits, work environments, and work relations are a key element in our overall stress management strategy.

SOURCES OF JOB STRESS

Just about any work situation can be a potential source of stress. The way we perceive our working environment determines, to an extent, the degree to which we're stressed and whether or not we'll experience serious stress symptoms.

In order to establish :60 second stress management procedures and handle job stress more effectively, we first must be able to recognize the things about our work that cause pressure. The following are ten of the most common job-related stress factors. Many of us will have others beside those that are listed. Recognizing the ones that affect us personally is an important first step.

- Disorganization or inability to manage time

- Conflict with supervisors or colleagues

- Unqualified to do the job

- Feeling overwhelmed or overburdened by work

- Too much or too little responsibility

- Inability to meet deadlines

- Unable to adapt to changes in work routine

- Inability to utilize skills

- Feeling of boredom

- No support from superiors

If we find ourselves locked into a working situation in which we cannot make changes or decisions that will eliminate specific job stress factors, we must practice attitude and behavior modification exercises. We also should take time to learn relaxation techniques and time management strategies.

The first step, however, is to identify and write down any aspect of our work that leads to stress symptoms. We should undertake this task in exactly the same manner as our daily stress diary. Job stress is, after all, just another stress. Remember, no matter what the stress, recognizing the symptoms, identifying the sources and setting specific goals to eliminate and relieve the sources are the three important steps in establishing :60 second management techniques.

JOB STRESS IN
THE 21ST CENTURY

One of the single biggest sources of physical and emotional stress is job loss or job insecurity, especially for individuals with families to care for and mortgages to pay. Even in good times when jobs are more secure, as much as 10 percent of the workforce can suffer from undiagnosed and untreated depression. In today's competitive and economically uncertain world, it's even worse. Greater expectations, longer office hours, work overload and increased pressures to get ahead and stay employed are driving some workers over the edge. Add to that an economy that is becoming more and more service-oriented and specialized plus the average worker's fears of falling behind or getting laid off and the stress can become almost paralyzing.

During the past few years, workplace stress has soared. With corporate scandals bankrupting companies, unemployment rising, the stock market stumbling and retirement accounts dwindling, it's little wonder that stress and burnout are costing employers millions in health care costs. To keep from joining the ranks of the jobless, the stressed-out and the depressed, here are some tips to make life in the twenty-first century workforce a bit easier.

- **Never be satisfied doing only what's expected.** Good employees and employers who appreciate them, know that if you do only 5 percent more than what you're expected to, you'll be doing more than 95 percent of your competition.

- **Keep up with changes.** Going to classes, conferences and other educational activities is one of the best ways to demonstrate that you're willing to put in extra effort. Let your record speak for itself. When lay-offs are necessary, the choice will be obvious. Those who constantly update their skills are those who end up staying with the company or getting promoted for their efforts.

- **Retrain for a change in career.** The days when most employees stay with the same company or the same career throughout life are over. By taking evening classes and learning new skills, you can make yourself much more marketable if you ever have to change careers. Also, by not waiting until the last minute to begin your reeducation, you'll be ready and able to start your new job search with a full and varied list of talents if there is an unexpected layoff.

- **Maintain a stable and normal family life.** Don't make your job search or retraining a twenty-four-hour, seven-day-a-week proposition. Make a daily or weekly schedule of resume sub-missions, calls and company research and stick with it. After that, spend time with your spouse and family, leaving your job hunting behind.

- **Notify your creditors and lenders.** If the unthinkable hap-pens and you lose your job, by arranging flexible or temporary payment plans or consolidating credit, you will lessen the stress that a sudden loss of income brings.

- **Take care of your health.** Individuals who don't exercise, lack sleep and eat poorly will develop stress-related illnesses and depression that affect their work and marketability more read-ily than those who are good to themselves. Conversely, individ-uals who eat well and maintain a daily exercise regimen will feel more confident and have more energy to keep up with the emotional drain of job hunting.

EXPECTATION VS.
REALITY

There's no such thing as a perfect job. Whatever career we choose, whatever job we do, there always will be the problem of altering or adjusting our expectations to meet reality. This need most often arises when we get our first job, when we change jobs or when we get pro-moted. Our enthusiasm and eagerness for work quickly disappears when the reality of work and the problems associated with it begin to surface. Sometimes we find that instead of the exciting, rewarding occupation we expected, in reality, our jobs might be downright dull. Whenever our expectations exceed job reality, but don't reach a bal-ance after a certain period of time, we begin to experience the stress of "unattainable expectations." Here's an example of how some expecta-tions and job realities can differ and become a real source of job stress.

EXPECTATION
Work will be challenging,
stimulating and rewarding.

REALITY
Work is more often a routine and
can be a very boring experience.

We'll be asked to use all our
educational training or all
our skills to do our job.

Much of what we learn in school
is not practiced on the job. We
often must learn to do things the
company way.

We'll be needed to utilize
our abilities and intelligence
in decision making and in
implementing new ideas.

Decision making and the
implementing of ideas are left to
senior executives and managers.

These are only some of the ways expectations and realities don't
match up in the real world. The first thing we need to realize is that
the standards we set for ourselves are sometimes too high, even for
good companies to meet. Being reasonable in what we expect from our
work in terms of compensation and emotional reward will make our
adjustment to reality much easier. If we're not, the stress of unattainable expectations can easily lead to deflated enthusiasm, cynicism,
total job dissatisfaction and burnout. These, in turn, can cause serious job-stress related illnesses such as ulcers, hypertension and coronary heart disease.

When reality finally sets in, how can we cope with the fact that our
expectations may never be realized? Instead of becoming depressed
and isolated, we can begin to adjust to reality by accepting three
irrefutable facts of work life:

1. Expectations in all areas of life, including work, are almost
   always distortions of reality. Reality, then, will always be a dis-
   appointment at first unless we accept the challenge and do
   something positive about it.

2. In almost all instances, work is something we need to fit into,
   not the other way around. Rare are the employers who will
   mold jobs to meet our personal needs or demands. Positive
   attitudes make us more flexible and allow us to fit into almost
   any situation we want.

3. No jobs, regardless of what they are, will satisfy us unless we
   adopt attitudes and behaviors that condition us to perceive job

events the way we want to perceive them. We can choose to make work either a pleasant or unpleasant experience through the power of our minds. We can lower our expectations and still receive satisfaction from our work by setting realistic goals and by coming to terms with our negative feelings and attitudes.

Our job expectations, then, can be as powerful as our perceptions, and just as easily changed through hard work. If we expect something good to happen and it doesn't, we naturally perceive our job situation in a negative way. If we set our expectations so high that we never attain what we expect, we begin to condition ourselves to perceive work and ourselves in a negative way all the time. We build subconscious images that reinforce and shape our attitudes and behavior, and we eventually form habits that strengthen our negative feelings toward work. Bringing expectations in line with reality can be difficult, but if we condition ourselves to perceive and accept job reality in a constructive way, we can avoid the pitfalls of chronic stress and burnout.

BURNOUT

The term "burnout" is often used these days whenever we talk about job stress, because it has become a major problem in many professional and nonprofessional occupations. Burnout, simply put, is a gradual process by which a once productive and committed worker loses all concern and interest in his or her job or profession. Victims of burnout often experience physical and emotional exhaustion, total lack of interest in work and detachment from fellow workers. Burnout isn't really the same as stress; rather, it's the direct result of prolonged exposure to stressful work conditions and situations.

Although burnout can strike anyone, the individuals most vulnerable are the ones who deal with people on a daily basis.

HIGH RISK
BURNOUT OCCUPATIONS

Although anyone in any profession can experience burnout, certain fields are especially vulnerable. These professions are health care, law enforcement and education.

Many of the stress symptoms exhibited by different high-risk groups are similar and even if you are not a member of any of these professions, you can still benefit from the suggestions. You may well be able to identify with the problems experienced by high-risk individuals.

Physicians

The greatest sources of emotional upheaval for physicians are therapeutic failures, diagnostic difficulties, deaths of young patients and experiencing adverse family impacts. When these negative events become unbearable, some doctors may even contemplate suicide. Recent studies show that male physicians, as a group, are twice as suicide-prone as the general population.

For some physicians, it is difficult to deal with a dual standard between their work and home environments. After being treated with awe and respect at work, for example, a physician may become angry and resentful when asked to take the garbage out or help do some laundry. This sudden drop in status can be difficult to cope with for individuals who are literally responsible for people's lives.

Physicians need to take immediate steps in order to keep from plunging deep into burnout. Some specific stress managements for physicians are:

1. *Learn time management techniques*

2. *Schedule shorter rotations during intense work conditions*

3. *Increase vacation time and time away from work*

4. *Vary daily routines*

5. *Become involved in outside activities and organizations*

6. *Exercise*

7. *Seek out support networks with other physicians*

Nurses

Nurses also experience burnout—but for different reasons. They not only are forced to deal with demanding patients but with stressed-out physicians as well. This dual source of stress is often the reason why nurses feel overburdened, overworked and under-appreciated.

Young nurses begin their careers with unusual enthusiasm and idealism, believing that nursing is a very special profession. When they begin to encounter critical, demanding and ungrateful patients or physicians who threat them like second-class citizens, their idealism is often shattered. One of the biggest reasons for rapid burnout in nurses is the disparity between expectation and reality.

Quick solutions are necessary to ease burnout. One study showed that nurses practicing relaxation techniques for as little as twenty minutes a day had a much better ability to cope with stress, a marked improvement in anxiety levels, an increase in their work energy and greater job satisfaction than those who didn't. Specific stress techniques nurses can use are:

1.   *Adjust work schedules and temper the care of dying or critically ill patients with other less serious cases*

2.   *Get involved in outside activities or volunteer work unrelated to health care*

3.   *Take time off to go on trips or just to relax*

4.   *Exercise*

5.   *Maintain regular sleep patterns*

Police Officers

Stress-related disorders among police officers include various physical ailments, emotional and personal problems and impaired work performance. Physical disorders range from backaches, muscle cramps and headaches to asthma, high blood pressure, heartburn and ulcers. Studies also have found high rates of coronary heart disease and digestive disorders. Emotional and personal problems include divorce, alcoholism, depression and suicide.

The very nature of police work, which often emphasizes authoritarianism and depersonalization, can cause police officers to feel isolated and lonely. This, in turn, can easily lead to aggressive behavior, apathy, cynicism, disobedience to regulations and withdrawal from the public and coworkers.

Some specific stress relaxation techniques for police officers are:

1.   *Develop or find a social support group that includes other police officers*

2.   *Take time off from police work completely*

3.   *Seek counseling at times of serious distress*

4.   *Do volunteer work within the community*

This last strategy is a key element in eliminating hostility and suspicion toward police officers within their own communities. Since hostility and suspicion often are responsible for creating the isolation, withdrawal and loneliness leads to burnout in police officers, active involvement in the communities that these heroes protect can be a great way to cope.

Teachers

When we hear the word burnout, many of us immediately think of the teaching profession. Teacher burnout is a critical issue that should be of concern to our entire society. Because it directly affects our children, whether it happens in kindergarten or high school, teacher burnout influences the attitudes children have toward education and, more importantly, the enthusiasm they have about learning. If children are confronted with teacher burnout early in their educational career, it may cause them to develop negative feelings about the entire school experience. If it occurs in the upper grades, it can create an apathetic and tense atmosphere in which older children are stifled at a time in their lives when the learning process can become especially vulnerable to negative reinforcement. Regardless of when it occurs, teacher burnout will invariably affect children by causing intensely negative feelings about education in general.

As with other professions in which burnout is common, teachers often encounter the same problem in finding that their expectations differ greatly from day-to-day reality. Young teachers graduate from college idealistic and energetic, ready to be the best educators they can be and wanting to make a life-long impact on children's lives. It is precisely because of this idealism that they often blame themselves for not being able to improve a system they see as failing their students. Instead of realizing their expectations, teachers quickly encounter the realities of under funding, cynicism, disinterest and graft that plague our educational system. They lose their enthusiasm for work, experience deep and profound job dissatisfaction and end up feeling cynical and frustrated.

Comprehensive burnout management for teachers requires goals that put school life back into perspective, so that the reality of the classroom is approached in a positive manner.

Some specific stress-relaxation techniques for teachers are:

1. *Continue to improve work skills.* Taking classes, attending seminars and participating in extra job training will prevent feelings of inadequacy.

2. *Schedule down time.* Coffee breaks and lunches shouldn't be used for grading papers or reading reports. Teachers need time away from school duties.

3. *Keep abreast of new ideas.* Using the same class notes and materials year after year will invariably lead to boredom and burnout on the part of teacher and student. By updating lesson plans and notes, teachers can stay interested in teaching and create a dynamic and interesting classroom environment for their charges.

4. *Form teacher support groups.* Communicate with and exchange ideas with fellow workers.

5. *Become a time-management expert.* A great deal of teacher burnout results from an inability to manage time effectively. As projects grow too large to handle and responsibilities become overwhelming, it is imperative for teachers to effectively implement time management strategies.

It is not only the workers in these specific job fields who need to be especially wary of symptoms that indicate early warnings of burnout syndrome. Other jobs that promote burnout are ones in which workers do repetitive or routine tasks, do not receive positive feedback or have great responsibility but little control. Some of the types of individuals most susceptible to burnout syndrome are perfectionists, egotists, idealists and workaholics.

BURNOUT RATING QUIZ

The following quiz is one way to rate how prone we are to burnout. In effect, it is a measure of our "burnout index." Following the quiz is a scoring key and a list of common signs and symptoms that are associated with burnout or that are seen shortly prior to burnout.

	Seldom	Some- times	Always
1. I feel hostile or angry at work.	1	2	3
2. I feel like I have to succeed all the time.	1	2	3
3. I find myself withdrawing from co-workers.	1	2	3

4. I feel like everything I'm asked to do is an imposition.   1   2   3

5. I find myself increasingly insensitive or callous to clients, co-workers or associates.   1   2   3

6. Work has become very boring, tedious and routine.   1   2   3

7. I feel like I'm at a standstill in my career.   1   2   3

8. I find myself feeling negative about work and focusing only on its bad aspects.   1   2   3

9. I find myself accomplishing less than I ever have before.   1   2   3

10. I have trouble organizing my work and time.   1   2   3

11. I'm more short-tempered that I've ever been before.   1   2   3

12. I feel inadequate and powerless to make changes at work.   1   2   3

13. I find myself taking out my work frustrations at home.   1   2   3

14. I consciously avoid personal contact more than I ever have.   1   2   3

15. I find myself asking whether my job is right for me.   1   2   3

16. I find myself thinking negatively about work even when I go to bed.   1   2   3

17. I approach each workday with the attitude of "I don't know if I'm going to make it through another day."   1   2   3

18. I feel as if no one at work cares   1   2   3
     about what I do.

19. I find myself spending less time   1   2   3
     working and more time avoiding
     work.

20. I feel tired or exhausted at work even   1   2   3
     when I get enough sleep at night.

Scoring Key: 20-34
                   No burnout

                   35-49
                   Moderate Burnout (early warning signs)

                   50-60
                   Severe Burnout (need help and guidance)

SIGNS AND SYMPTOMS OF BURNOUT

Absenteeism	Hostility
Alcoholism	Indifference
Anxiety	Insensitivity
Apathy	Irritability
Boredom	Isolation
Callousness	Job dissatisfaction
Conflicts with workers	Low morale
Cynicism	Malaise
Defensiveness	Marital problems
Disillusionment	Moodiness
Depersonalization	Negativism
Depression	Paranoia
Drug dependence	Pessimism
Exhaustion	Reduced accomplishments
Family problems	Resentment
Fatigue	Sexual problems
Fault finding	Suicide thoughts
Frustration	Weakness
Hopelessness	Withdrawal

If we're on the road to burnout, we'll probably experience several of these symptoms before the final stage of burnout occurs. But no matter what the cause, burnout always involves a pattern that leaves us de-energized and emotionally exhausted.

Burnout is essentially the result of unrelieved job stress. When we feel trapped in a job or helpless to solve problems or conflicts, the unforeseen and unwelcome realities of our situation cause frustration, anxiety and a feeling of powerlessness. This frustration is often transmitted to the people we work with and results in a work environment that becomes unbearable and depersonalized for everyone.

Nancy was a young nurse who graduated near the top of her class. She brought with her a genuine and enthusiastic desire to help her patients and was eager to do everything she could to become an ideal nurse. After all, as a youngster, Nancy had been taught to see a glamorous and idealistic vision of nursing and she continued to have that picture in her mind while in school. Shortly after she began work, however, she encountered critical and ungrateful patients and physicians who treated her like a servant, not a professional. Her expectations were shattered. Gradually, Nancy began to develop negative attitudes about patients and doctors, became hostile and short-tempered and started to withdraw from her co-workers. In the end, Nancy became so bitter, cynical, angry and dissatisfied that she was a threat to the health of her patients.

There are four stages of burnout syndrome. We need to be aware of each stage in order to recognize the warning signals that tell us that danger lies ahead.

Nancy went through these four stages before she finally burned herself out completely. Had she caught the burnout during the first three stages, it is possible that she could have reversed the process and become a happy, productive worker again. Very few individuals, however, can reverse the burnout process entirely once they've remained in the fourth and final stage of burnout for any length of time.

FOUR STAGES OF
BURNOUT SYNDROME

Stage 1. High Expectations and Idealism
       Symptoms: Enthusiasm about the job
                         Dedication and commitment to work
                         High energy levels and accomplishments
                         Positive and constructive attitudes
                         Good outlook

Stage 2.   Pessimism and Early Job Dissatisfaction
Symptoms: Physical and mental fatigue
            Frustration and disillusionment
            Lowered morale
            Boredom
            Early stress symptoms

Stage 3.   Withdrawal and Isolation
Symptoms: Avoiding contact with co-workers
            Anger and hostility
            Severe negativism
            Depression and other emotional distress
            Inability to think or concentrate
            Extreme physical and mental fatigue
            Excessive amounts of stress symptoms

Stage 4.   Irreversible Detachment and Loss of Interest
Symptoms: Very low self-esteem
            Chronic absenteeism
            Terminally negative feelings about work
            Total cynicism
            Inability to interact with others
            Serious emotional distress
            Severe physical and emotional stress
            symptoms

ELEVEN :60 SECOND
BURNOUT
"EXTINGUISHERS"

Unless we've gone into the fourth and final stage of burnout, we can reverse the process through simple changes in our job goals, attitudes and behaviors. Here are some very effective coping strategies—proven burnout extinguishers—that will lead to :60 second management techniques:

1. *Express feelings and emotions.* Putting stress into words through communication with colleagues can prevent the isolation that is often felt during the later stages of burnout. The exchange of ideas acts as a buffer because sharing and communicating has a unique way of relieving stress and putting things in perspective.

2. *Schedule downtime.* Everyone needs breaks away from work. Instead of using lunch or coffee breaks to catch up on unfinished or extra work, spend downtime doing something completely unrelated to work. Time off is absolutely essential in refreshing attitudes and job outlook.

3. *Recognize energy patterns and schedule work accordingly.* During a normal work day, we all have high and low levels of energy. Finding out when high energy levels occur and then scheduling stressful duties only during those times will prevent wear out and energy loss.

4. *Never schedule more than one stressful activity at the same time.* This may take some thought and planning beforehand, but putting up with only one stressful situation at any given time will prevent work pileup, make you feel like you're accomplishing more and relieve the stress of feeling overworked.

5. *Engage in regular physical activity.* It's very important to participate in physical exercise because stimulating the body refreshes the mind. Our brain requires activity in the rest of our body to revitalize the senses and enhance performance. Exercise also builds physical resistance to fatigue and illness and makes us feel better about ourselves. When stagnation sets in, resistance and energy are lowered and the natural tendency is to become more susceptible to physical and emotional distress.

6. *Break projects down into smaller parts.* Some of us have a tendency to become overwhelmed by a project soon after we start it. By cutting a big project down to its individual components, it never looks as difficult or overwhelming. We can then tackle it piece by piece and never even realize how big it is until it's finally done.

7. *Delegate responsibility.* If we're ever in a position to delegate responsibility to others, we should make it a point to do so. Rather than take on every problem that comes up, we need to allow others to share in problem solving and decision making.

8. *Learn to say no.* Never feel obligated to take on extra assignments or do special projects which aren't required but nevertheless cause feelings of anger and hostility. Saying yes all the

time can make us feel helpless to control our own workload, while being able to say no gives us a feeling of control and satisfaction. Keep in mind, this isn't the same as not wanting to get involved and be committed. Giving ourselves the choice of what we want to be involved in or committed to is the kind of control we need to become stress-free.

9. *Improve work skills.* We need to become more aware of new changes and keep abreast of current technologies and ideas. Taking classes, going to seminars and participating in extra job training will keep us up-to-date and prevent feelings of inadequacy and unpreparedness. If we don't, we'll become more and more withdrawn and isolated from our jobs' requirements and our coworkers. Eventually, our inability to work effectively with technology and with others can cause serious emotional problems.

10. *Strive for success.* Never be satisfied with doing only what you've been trained to do. Successful individuals learn new things, take risks, go out of their way to improve career goals and are anxious to vitalize their lives by meeting new and exciting challenges. If you're willing to extend yourself and reach for success, then chances are you'll never experience burnout.

11. *Learn to relax.* Set aside some time each day to bring your body back to a state of "relaxed equilibrium." Learning the art of conscious relaxation (discussed in a later chapter) will have a greater benefit than sleep and allow you to accept and cope with stressful situations more readily.

Two myths about burnout are that it occurs suddenly and that it only happens to workers in certain occupations. In reality, burnout can happen to anyone. It usually develops slowly and can take years before the symptoms of burnout manifest themselves as physical and emotional problems, but left unchecked it can do severe damage.

The good news is that it's easily recognizable and easily reversible during the first several stages. Dealing with burnout, however, requires both preventive action and active stress reduction. Practicing the coping strategies discussed in this chapter attacks the root of job stress and job dissatisfaction caused by attitudes and behaviors. Using the relaxation techniques discussed in later chapters together with these coping strategies will make it easier to reverse the burnout process and help you experience a fuller and more rewarding work life.

· Chapter 5 ·

Time Management

One of the biggest stress factors we face, whether it's at work or at home, is our inability to manage time properly. Having the time to do the things we want to do is important, but can be difficult to achieve in this increasingly fast-paced world. Hence, proper time-management skills are essential. Without them, we experience stress, because if we don't have enough time, we lose the freedom to do what needs to be done, to be who we want to be and to enjoy the things we want to do. We accomplish only what we can fit into our schedules. And we find ourselves pressured and stressed because our lives and our work are constantly dictated by time.

Time management, then, allows us to organize our lives in a way that makes us happier and more productive. It gives us the ability to schedule ourselves into a normal day-to-day routine so we're left with the time we need for ourselves and our family. It prevents chronic stress by eliminating the constraints we place on ourselves as a result of poor or inadequate organizational skills.

The following time quiz should help identify trouble spots and guide us toward our goal of becoming successful time managers. Read each statement carefully and circle the corresponding number that comes "closest" to answering the statement. (1 = Always; 2 = Usually; 3 = Sometimes; 4 = Rarely). Add up your score with the scoring key after the quiz, which indicates levels of time management skills.

1. I find that I have enough time   1   2   3   4
for myself—to do the things I
enjoy doing.

2. I'm aware of deadlines and   1   2   3   4
   schedule my work to meet them
   in plenty of time.

3. I write down specific objectives   1   2   3   4
   in order to work toward goals.

4. I use a calendar to write down   1   2   3   4
   appointments, deadlines, things
   to do, general notes.

5. I feel in control of time while   1   2   3   4
   at work and at home.

6. I plan and schedule my time on a   1   2   3   4
   weekly and/or monthly basis.

7. I make a daily to-do list and refer   1   2   3   4
   to it several times per day.

8. I set priorities in order of   1   2   3   4
   importance and then schedule
   time around them.

9. I'm able to find blocks of time   1   2   3   4
   when I need them in case
   something important or extra
   has to be fit in.

10. I'm able to say no when I'm   1   2   3   4
    pressed for time.

11. I try to delegate responsibility to   1   2   3   4
    others in order to make more time
    for myself.

12. I organize my desk and work   1   2   3   4
    area to prevent clutter and
    confusion.

13. I find it easy to eliminate or   1   2   3   4
    reschedule low priority items.

14. I try to do things in a way that   1   2   3   4
     cuts down on duplicated effort.

15. I find that doing everything   1   2   3   4
     myself is very inefficient.

16. I try to shift priorities as soon   1   2   3   4
     as they change.

17. I find it easy to identify sources   1   2   3   4
     of time problems.

18. I find it easy to eliminate or   1   2   3   4
     reshuffle unnecessary paperwork.

19. My meetings and activities are   1   2   3   4
     well organized and efficient.

20. I know what I'm capable of and   1   2   3   4
     try not to overextend myself.

21. I find it easy to keep up with   1   2   3   4
     changes that affect my schedule
     or workload.

22. I know what my responsibilities   1   2   3   4
     and duties are.

23. I try to schedule the most difficult   1   2   3   4
     work during my most productive
     times.

24. I try to get only the pertinent   1   2   3   4
     information before making a
     decision rather than trying to get
     as much information as possible.

25. I finish one job or task   1   2   3   4
     before going on to the next.

Scoring key: 25-40=Excellent time manager
                   41-55=Good time manager
                   56-100=Poor time manager

After completing the quiz, we need to go back and identify those areas that are the most consistent sources of time-related stress. By recognizing the specific behavior patterns and attitudes that interfere with our ability to organize, manage and schedule time, we can begin to reverse time management problems quickly and effectively. The most common areas to look for are:

- Not prioritizing tasks

- Not scheduling daily, weekly, or monthly activities

- Not delegating responsibility

- Not being able to say no

- Not writing down objectives in order to meet deadlines

- Not using a calendar to organize commitments

- Not shifting priorities to make room for more urgent tasks

- Not reducing clutter and unnecessary paperwork

- Not being able to give up total control

- Not being able to avoid procrastination

These are only the most common areas of poor time management. We all have our own individual weaknesses and, therefore, we need to recognize and eliminate those weaknesses by writing them down in a time management diary. The four areas that should be included in our diary are:

1. The event or activity.

2. Its priority ranking.
   1 = important
   2 = less important

3 = least important

4 = not important at all

3. The action we take.

4. A strategy for improving the way we handle the event or activity in order to enhance time management skills.

TIME MANAGEMENT
DIARY

A week of writing down activities and actions should be enough to indicate where time problems lie and what sorts of strategies we can take to eliminate wasted effort. At the end of each day, write down specific instances of "timewasters" you encounter and make a list of strategies that will solve problems dealing with those timewasters.

Keeping a diary of activities and an accurate record of timewasters should give us a clear picture of how we're doing as time managers and how far we need to go to become ideal time managers. It's impossible to practice time management without first knowing what it is that makes us unable to accomplish a certain amount of work in a given amount of time. Once we put our fingers on our problem areas and their sources, we can begin to adjust our daily behavior patterns in order to eliminate the roots of our time-related stress. This is where conditioning and habit formation come into play once again. By consciously practicing good time management activities, we'll begin to break our old time management habits and condition ourselves to develop new and more effective behavior patterns. Here's an example of a time-management diary:

Time	Activity	Priority Ranking	Action Taken	Improvement Strategy
7:00				
7:30				
8:00				
8:30				

Time	Activity	Priority Ranking	Action Taken	Improvement Strategy
9:00				
9:30				
10:00				
10:30				
11:00				
12:00				
12:30				
1:00				
1:30				
2:00				
2:30				
3:00				
3:30				
4:00				
4:30				
5:00				

Time	Activity	Priority Ranking	Action Taken	Improvement Strategy
6:00				
6:30				
7:00				
7:30				
8:00				
8:30				
9:00				
9:30				
10:00				

FIFTEEN :60 SECOND
TIME MANAGEMENT
STRATEGIES

The recurring theme of conditioning and habit formation is a powerful force in shaping our :60 second stress management techniques and time management is no different. The positive reinforcer of good time management is a rewarding and satisfying experience. The more effectively we manage our time, the less stress we will feel and the more positive the conditioning process becomes. Eventually, good time management will become a permanent and natural :60 second reaction to stress.

Time Waster	Strategy
Looking through every piece of mail	Discard junk mail immediately. Put low-priority mail aside until more time is available.
Having meetings that go on for a long time	Make a meeting agenda and don't go beyond a specific time limit. Prepare more thoroughly to avoid unnecessary delays.
Having a lot of small duties that interfere with more important tasks	Prioritize duties and/or delegate some of the lesser responsibilities to others. Eliminate unnecessary tasks.

Of course, nothing comes easily at first and our ingrained habits prevent us from becoming ideal time managers overnight. Only through repetition can we shape our behavior in the manner we choose. Here are fifteen ways to develop good time management habits and achieve our number one goal of automatic :60 second management stress relaxation techniques:

1. *Write down weekly goals, plans, activities and objectives.* This kind of a tentative to-do list will get the wheels rolling and make further planning and scheduling easier.

2. *Prioritize tasks according to importance.* After writing down these activities, give them a priority ranking: top, high, low or least.

3. *Plan schedules in an organized manner by using a calendar or appointment book.* These tools are organized in ways that make scheduling and planning easy, effective and manageable.

4. *Schedule demanding tasks during periods of high energy.* There are morning, noon and night people. Scheduling in this manner will allow you to do your best on the most important assignments.

5. *Eliminate time wasting activities.* Eliminate all the things you do every day that are unnecessary. Put them at the end of the list.

6. *Delegate authority.* One of the biggest causes of stress comes

from the attitude that you have to do it all yourself. Take a look at your schedule and decide what can be handled by someone else.

7. *Finish one task before starting another.* Some of us can handle several things at the same time; most of us can't. Assign a priority rating to each task and eliminate the tendency to procrastinate.

8. *Write it down.* Taking good notes supplies you with information, reminds you of priorities and provides you with a backup to your calendar. Always keep a pencil and small not pad available and get in the habit of using it.

9. *Learn to say no.* Of all time management techniques, learning to say no is one of the best :60 second ways to avoid scheduling problems, eliminate time wasting activities and stay in control of day-to-day planning.

10. *Leave some of your schedule open.* Never fill up your schedule completely. By leaving yourself available time for emergency meetings or unexpected jobs, you'll be less anxious about your ability to schedule "just one more thing."

11. *Develop and keep deadlines.* Don't put off projects. Procrastination just makes deadlines harder to meet. Know when your deadlines are and keep them.

12. *Don't put off making decisions.* Effective decision making doesn't necessarily mean waiting until you have every fact and figure. Write down the decision you have to make, list the primary facts and figures that you need, get them as quickly as possible and make your decision.

13. *Improve reading and writing skills.* Effective communication, including the ability to read quickly and write coherently, is basic to all effective time management.

14. *Develop an effective reminder system.* No one can remember everything. Without a reminder, follow-up material and attention to small details suffer.

15. *Be in control.* Being in control is as important in time manage-

ment as in stress management. In any time management situation, the telephone can be your worst enemy. Avoid unnecessary calls or long conversations. If at all possible, avoid answering your own phone. Avoid unnecessary socializing. Avoid getting involved in events not concerned with your job. Avoid unorganized meetings or discussions.

It's not the things we do during the day that create time problems. It is the way we do them. More often than not, the reasons for our inability to manage time are improper behavior patterns and attitudes. However, behavior and attitudes can be changed through proper techniques and conditioning and both can be used as positive reinforcers that make us more efficient at utilizing the time we have.

· Chapter 6 ·

Stress and Mental Health

Throughout history, mental health problems have been depicted in stories about people being "possessed by demons" and acting in an "ungodly and unnatural way." The stigma of being different in thought and action from the general population was so great that mental health was largely ignored or hidden behind closed doors for much of our history. But with rapid modernization came increasing anxiety, depression and psychoses and we began to look more closely at mental health disorders. We learned that in some cases, mental illness was linked to the stresses we ourselves had created. Stress is now regarded as one of the main causes of mental and emotional problems.

The reasons individuals develop mental health disorders are complex and it would be simplistic to attribute all mental health problems to stress alone, but mental health and stability can be affected deeply by the way we handle stress. Certain coping strategies are vital tools that can be used to fight the emotional traumas and mental disorders caused by prolonged exposure to stress.

DEPRESSION

Psychiatrists consider many kinds of depression to be a response to emotional stress rather than a specific disease or illness. Treatment varies depending on the healthcare professional, but many use individual coping strategies and various stress management techniques. We all become depressed at one time or another and we all exhibit different signs and symptoms of depression. Depression can be something as simple as an extended sadness or something as severe as deep withdrawal. Here is a list of common symptoms that can be used as a guide to recognizing certain traits and behaviors of depression:

- Insomnia or excessive sleep

- Compulsive behavior (overeating, anorexia, bulimia, etc.)

- Withdrawal and isolation

- Loss of control

- Loss of memory and/or concentration

- Disinterest in work or other activities

- Physical pains (headaches, backaches, etc.)

- Feelings of loneliness and/or emptiness

- Frequent self-doubts and self-criticism

- Irritability

- Excessive alcohol or drug abuse

- Loss of interest in sex

- Thoughts of or attempts at suicide

- Enduring feelings of sadness, guilt, or hopelessness

When we look at specific examples of mental health problems, we discover that stressful, negative life events account for a large number of depression cases. Many studies have clearly demonstrated that depressed individuals experience stressful life events in the months that precede the start of their depression.

One does not have to suffer a cataclysmic stressful event. Rather, in many cases, the stress events that cause depression are small, repetitive occurrences. The cumulative effects of repetitive stress can be equally, if not more, potent than a major traumatic event.

If there's one positive side to depression, however, it's that in almost every case, it's easy to recognize. Early warning signals allow us to confront our stress immediately and effectively before depression slips into a dangerous and chronic stage.

FOUR :60 SECOND
STRESS MANAGEMENTS
FOR DEPRESSION

Unless depression is severe and caused by deeply rooted emotional problems or a chemical imbalance, certain coping strategies can be used to reverse or lessen depressive symptoms. Here are four :60 second managements for depression:

1. *Increase social contacts and interactions with friends and family.* Take :60 seconds to make a list of people you enjoy being with. Make an effort to broaden your circle of friends and see them on a regular basis. Stress and depression decrease as interactions increase.

2. *Improve communication between yourself and others.* This is especially true of verbal communication between family members and loved ones. Communication opens doors, makes relationships grow and relieves stress. Take :60 seconds to really listen to the person with whom you're speaking.

3. *Develop social support systems.* Social support systems may include a group of friends, your community, your church or your family. Simply surrounding yourself with others can greatly brighten your outlook on life.

4. *Get involved.* Taking part in activities, events, organizations and social groups will get your mind off the source of your stress. Many depressed individuals discover that involvement alone is not only the answer to their stress, but also many of their social and emotional problems.

The best treatment for depression really depends on the personality and character of the individual and the extent of depression. Often, a professional counselor or psychiatrist is needed to help decide which treatment plan is best.

SCHIZOPHRENIA

Schizophrenia is actually a group of mental disorders related to the thinking process. It includes symptoms such as delusions, hallucinations and extreme withdrawal from society and other people. Like depression, schizophrenia may have a number of different causes, including environmental factors and genetic predisposition. In many cases, however, people on the verge of schizophrenia have been shown to experience severely stressful events which precipitate the disorder.

In the past, stress wasn't even considered a factor in the development of schizophrenia. It is now believed that individuals who are vulnerable to schizophrenia may succumb to it because stress actually precipitates it. And even though many cases of schizophrenia are caused by factors other than stress, we can't ignore the fact that stressful life events are commonly found prior to the onset of the disease itself. Standard therapy usually involves the participation of family members, relatives and social support groups.

The emotional stress associated with being the parent, spouse or relative of a schizophrenic can be even greater than the stress experienced by the schizophrenic. Because of this, the benefits of support groups for family members are enormous. In these groups, stress is relieved by putting problems into words and sharing them. Often, potentially high-tension events are defused, because individuals are once again able to cope with situations that they couldn't deal with alone. Social support is an important part of schizophrenia treatment for both the sufferer and his or her loved ones, because it involves relationships and activities that act as buffers against stressful life events.

SEXUAL DYSFUNCTION

One of the leading causes of sexual problems is emotional stress. In many cases, simply recognizing the source of stress is enough to bring about complete recovery. On the other hand, failure to recognize stress as a cause can lead to serious emotional disorders and permanent loss of sexual desire.

In the male, both sex hormone and sperm production can be severely inhibited as a result of stressful experiences. Therefore, not only is the sex drive lowered, but fertility is significantly decreased. Sexual problems are especially stressful because they tend to spiral into a cycle that grows worse and worse over time. In order to avoid stress, couples begin to find ways to avoid intimacy and end up damaging their relationships.

Two important stress managements that can lead to a solution are:

1. *Communicate.* Anyone experiencing sexual problems can become lonely and hostile. Couples need to know that each individual must become a partner in the treatment of stress.

A man or woman alone can seldom overcome the cycle of sexual deficiency without cooperation from his or her partner. In many cases, the relief of sharing the stress, fear and anxiety is enough for complete recovery.

2. *Use special exercises to help reverse sexual problems.* There are several excellent books which discuss sexual problems, their causes and their cures. Don't be afraid to experiment.

Sexual problems in and of themselves are a tremendous source of stress. Becoming impotent or losing interest in sex can easily lead to depression and anxiety and cause illnesses such as ulcers, which may develop into more serious medical problems. It's impossible to say how many good marriages have broken up because couples didn't realize just how much stress had affected their sex lives. If there's one action we can take, it's to include our spouse or partners or be included by him or her in order to gain the strength needed to overcome a problem that can't be dealt with alone. It takes two to tango, so to speak.

Whenever we encounter a stress-related sexual problem, we need to remember three things: with high expectation comes occasional failure; with occasional failure should come understanding, compassion and a sense of unity and; with understanding and unity comes communication and a deeper awareness of one another's needs. It's only through understanding, compassion and communication that we can truly rid ourselves of sexual problems that are driven by negative stress responses. If we can do that, we'll experience the joy and satisfaction of finally knowing that sexual freedom lies not within the bounds of bedroom walls but within ourselves!

MENTAL HEALTH IN
VIETNAM VETERANS

The mental health problems of Vietnam veterans are unique in a number of ways. They've had to deal with the emotional trauma of participating not only in the unimaginable horrors of war, but in serving in a war that made them the brunt of hostility and criticism when they finally returned home. As a result, many men still suffer from severe emotional damage, as well as from the abuse they received when they finally returned home. Today, we view Vietnam veterans differently than we did in the past, but thousands of veterans still carry the emotional scars of rejection. They need the benefits of social support groups in order to cope with the stress in their lives.

This pattern of psychological stress in veterans also has been seen in previous wars. When we look at past mental health records, we find that during World War II as many as 500,000 individuals were discharged from the military for psychological reasons. It's not known how many of those veterans continued to have emotional problems—or how many continue to have emotional problems even today. Presumably, though, the number is high among those who completed their service and those who were discharged. The life-or-death situations in wartime are stressors beyond the imagination of anyone who has not lived through them.

When comparing the various types of coping strategies used for and by veterans, it was found that positive social support had the biggest influence in helping veterans deal with post-wartime stress. In some cases, intense psychiatric help is needed in order to alleviate severe stress disorders. In general, however, some of the most effective coping strategies are:

1. *Developing and mastering interpersonal relationships.* This can be done by using behavior and attitude modification to improve one's outlook; learning communication skills to interact with others; and participating in outside activities to develop a social support network.

2. *Joining veterans' groups and organizations.* Groups that include people with similar experiences are a good way to cope with stress, because you can "talk things out" with others who really know what you're going through.

3. *Using positive reinforcement strategies.* Reward-based programs can improve self-image, raise low self-esteem and condition the brain to respond in a positive and constructive way.

POST TRAUMATIC STRESS DISORDER (PTSD)

For decades, military health professionals have dealt with PTSD—formerly known as "shell shock" or "combat fatigue." Today, we know that anyone can experience PTSD, a complex syndrome resulting from an individual's experience with major life trauma. According to experts, the September 11 terrorist attacks have psychologically affected millions of people across the country, many of whom may still be suffering physically and emotionally as a result. Some of us may be affected for years to come.

The people who seem to have the most difficulty dealing with such traumas, besides those who lost friends and relatives, are our hardened first responders and those most delicate: police, fire, search and rescue workers and children. In fact, some studies have shown that children who were exposed to events like the space shuttle disaster, the Oklahoma City bombing, the Gulf War and the events of 9/11 solely through viewing them on television, experienced PTSD. In almost all cases of PTSD, the best way to cope is through social support and lots of contact with friends and relatives. Children do much better when parents speak to them about traumatic events and limit television viewing. If signs of PTSD do not dissipate within a few months, it may be necessary to see a psychologist.

SEASONAL AFFECTIVE
DISORDER (SAD)

Seasonal Affective Disorder (SAD) is a phenomenon in which individuals become depressed, sometimes severely, as a result of not being exposed to enough light. It is, of course, most common in the winter. Individuals with SAD are normally affected during the winter months when the photoperiod is shortest and in temporal geographic areas where the dark phase of the dark-light cycle is prolonged (Alaska, for example). The pineal gland, located in the brain, releases a hormone called melatonin, which we now know can alter moods and behavior. Melatonin is inhibited by a lack of light. Whenever levels of melatonin begin to decrease as a result of less frequent exposure to light, some individuals begin to suffer a series of symptoms that often are mistaken for depression or written of as "the winter blues." Symptoms of SAD vary from individual to individual, but according to experts, the most common symptoms include:

Sadness	Withdrawal from others
Depression	Increased periods of sleep
Irritability	Decreased sexual activity or desire
Anxiety	Increased appetite
Fatigue	Weight gain
Sluggishness	Craving for sweets
Restlessness	Moodiness

These symptoms may be continual throughout the fall and winter and disappear completely during the spring and summer months, though some SAD patients don't actually regain their full energy and activity levels until the summer months, when the photoperiod is longest. Increasing the short winter photoperiod by adding artificial bright light can reverse symptoms of SAD within a few days.

If you're affected by SAD, you may be able to reverse your symptoms by exposing yourself daily to a special fluorescent light, which must be much brighter than normal indoor illumination. The SunBox Company (www.sunbox.com) manufactures special, high-intensity fluorescent lighting, which is effective in curing over 80 percent of all SAD patients. Your physician is in the best position to diagnose SAD and can prescribe a daily treatment regimen that's right for you. He or she can also tell you how you can obtain the special light you need.

PREMENSTRUAL SYNDROME (PMS)

PMS remains a controversial subject, because no real, concrete evidence has been found to indicate its causes or even that it exists. Many experts, however, feel that PMS is linked to periodic hormonal changes and, thus, place it along with SAD and some forms of depression in the category of biorhythmic disorders. PMS also may be caused or triggered by changes in brain chemicals prior to menstruation or as a result of social or environmental factors such as severe stress events. Symptoms of PMS include:

Water retention	Lethargy and fatigue
Depression	Crying spells
Anger	Increased appetite
Irritability	Weight gain
Anxiety	Craving for sweets
Negativism	Emotional upheavals
Acne	Headaches

Most women notice at least some of these symptoms shortly before menstruation. PMS, however, refers to the more severe symptoms, in which women virtually can become disabled as a result of intense emotional, behavioral or physiological changes. Recent studies have shown that PMS can be treated with hormone therapy or with diuretics, but in many cases symptoms of PMS have been dramatically relieved with a combination of exercise, diet and changes in certain habits. The following are four important strategies that can be used to relieve PMS symptoms for many women.

1. Exercise regularly.
2. Maintain a well-balanced diet.
3. Cut down on caffeine.
4. Eliminate cigarettes and alcohol.

LONELINESS

In today's society, loneliness is often the result of detachment, divorce and our highly mobile society and does not necessarily stem from actual physical isolation.

According to experts, the key to overcoming loneliness is to reach out and give yourself the opportunity to grow with others as well as grow within yourself. There are several effective stress repressors leading to :60 second stress managements:

1. *Develop a wide variety of interests.* The worst thing you can do is sit and dwell on how lonely you feel and how few friends you have. Get out. No one has ever increased their circle of friends by avoiding contact with people.

2. *Become a volunteer.* By reaching out and serving others, you'll get your mind off your loneliness; keep busy, feel great about yourself and you will come to realize there are others less fortunate than yourself.

3. *Develop your introverted side.* It is important for you to learn to enjoy your own company, so that you don't feel an urgent need to be around others in order to keep from being lonely.

THE IMPORTANCE OF SLEEP

Based on numerous research findings, sleep is critical to maintain proper function of our physical and mental systems and in maintaining overall health and feelings of well-being. Without adequate sleep, most individuals tend to become irritable, moody, fatigued, sexually inactive, mentally confused, less resistant to colds and other infections and increasingly prone to more serious illnesses and disease. Research from Canada has shown that people with insomnia are more aggravated by minor stresses that pop up in daily life and rate their lives as more stressful than those who sleep well. "It's a vicious cycle," says Dr, Charles Morin of the University of Laval in Quebec. "People who have trouble dealing with stress may have trouble sleeping at night, which can then lead to poor attention, trouble concentrating and bad mood during the next day. Stress can cause insomnia, but insomnia can also aggravate daytime stress."

Anthropologists theorize that sleep evolved over a long period of time and its purpose was to protect our ancestors from dangers they might have encountered during the night. Psychologists and sleep researchers also believe that it's an evolutionary defense mechanism that restores the body after the wear and tear it goes through each day

Since the 1930s, sleep has been studied using the electroencephalogram (EEG) to determine the kinds of brain activities that are either present or being disrupted. Typically, a person passes through five main stages of sleep, each stage characterized by different brain waves. There are periods of the night called rapid eye movement sleep or REM and quieter periods called non-REM sleep stages. We spend about 25 percent of the night in REM and go through all five stages four or five times during a typical eight-hour sleep session. Each lasts about 30 minutes. The body is very relaxed, breathing slows and heart rate decreases.

It's a fact that people who sleep an average of eight hours per day live longer and better than people who spend very little time sleeping or those who sleep for prolonged periods each day. Furthermore, people with sleep disorders or people whose sleep patterns are always disrupted, like shift workers, suffer more illnesses and, statistically, tend to die at younger ages. Studies done on factory shift workers, for example, have shown that on average, they sleep two hours less per night than non-shift workers and have significantly less stage II and REM sleep. Because their sleep patterns are "fragmented," they always feel tired and are never able to recover from work.

While it may be true that we need less sleep as we get older, our sleep patterns need to be consistent for us to maintain good health. But it's not always easy to maintain good sleep habits as we age because our bodies change. Older individuals don't make brain chemicals in the same amount as younger individuals and as we get older, the brain doesn't respond to those chemicals as effectively. Since with age comes responsibility, we also have more things on our minds, we get stressed out by more complex issues, we become depressed more often and, as a result, the quality of our sleep suffers.

If obvious factors such as a neighbor's barking dog or a crying baby can be ruled out as the source of sleep deprivation, our inability to sleep may be the symptom of a more serious physical or emotional problem. If using the suggestions listed below doesn't work, one needs to consult a physician to determine if there's anything else wrong. Disrupted sleep patterns may be a sign of a chemical imbalance, clinical depression or some other disorder that prevents one from sleeping.

Any good prevention program involves not only adequate sleep but normal sleep patterns as well. It's not good to sleep eight hours one night, then five another, or go to bed at ten o'clock one evening and after midnight the next. Doing that is the surest way to disrupt one's biological clock and to fall into a pattern of insomnia. In most cases, we can improve sleep more effectively by ourselves than by using any sleeping pill a doctor would prescribe. The best treatment is always natural self-treatment.

Unless one has a physical problem that needs to be treated by a doctor, here are some effective ways to get back into normal sleep patterns and ensure that the body is recovering as well as possible:

- *Try, as much as possible, to go to bed at the same time every evening.* The worst thing anyone can do is to disrupt the body's natural clock by continually resetting it. By constantly changing the time we go to bed, we prevent our body from adjusting. The best way to get into a good sleep habit is to develop a ritual so that we can make the transition from day to night.

- *Wake up at the same time each morning.* Repetition trains the body to sleep well. Even if we stay up late or sleep in on weekends, we need to force ourselves not to go more than an extra hour or so before getting up.

- *Avoid afternoon naps.* Rather than making us feel refreshed, naps can cause normal nighttime sleep patterns to be disrupted and may ultimately make us feel even worse. To get out of the nap habit, we should go outside, take a walk or do something different. Within a few days, our body will forget that it needs that fifteen extra minutes of sleep

- *Avoid caffeine and caffeine-containing products before going to bed.* Coffee, with its high caffeine content, is the most notorious thief of sleep, but other products contain caffeine as well. Soft drinks, chocolate and certain medications may not contain as much caffeine as a cup of java, but they may contain just enough to keep us awake. For some people, the effects of caffeine may linger for as long as four to eight hours. Nicotine is an even more potent stimulant and one we should avoid altogether, but we should avoid it in the evening especially.

- *Don't participate in brain-stimulating activities before bedtime.* Some people assume that using their minds will tire them out and make them sleep better, but just the opposite happens. Our brain becomes over-stimulated and we end up thinking too many thoughts, causing us to toss and turn. There's a time for everything and the body needs to know when it's time for sleep, so we should never read, watch TV or do paperwork in bed. If we feel like we have to read, it's best to pick up something that will not make us turn pages.

- *Drink a warm cup of milk before bed.* Milk contains the essential amino acid tryptophan, which is converted to serotonin in the brain. Moderate increases in serotonin induce sleep. It's important, though, that we not eat prior to going to bed. The increased blood circulation caused by digestion will interfere with sleep

- *Avoid alcohol to induce sleep.* Although alcohol is a central nervous system depressant, it's a mistake to rely on a nightcap to get to sleep. First of all, people who depend on a drink every evening are conditioning themselves to become dependent on alcohol as the only way to be able to fall asleep. It's a bad habit to get into. And secondly, alcohol disrupts our normal sleep patterns, so while we may fall asleep initially, the sleep will not last and it will not be as deep or as restful as it would have been without the alcohol.

- *Maintain an exercise program, but don't exercise late in the evening.* Exercise increases blood circulation to the brain, which will keep us awake. It also triggers the release of adrenaline, the hormone responsible for increasing heart rate, breathing, oxygen consumption and blood pressure. The best time to exercise is in the morning, the afternoon or early evening.

- *Avoid nighttime activities that wake you up automatically.* Some individuals have a glass or two of water or a cup of hot tea right before bed. A few hours later they're waking up to go to the bathroom. While they're up, they may have another glass of water because they have become dehydrated. Done on a regular basis, this routine becomes so ingrained that the person subconsciously wakes up at a certain time and has a difficult time getting back to sleep.

- *Make sure that your bed or your mattress is not causing discomfort or backaches that disrupt sleep.* In many cases, simply getting a new or a different type of mattress does the trick. The best ones are a bit on the firm side, because they offer support and don't create bends in the body that will wake us up when we roll over.

- *Learn stress management relaxation techniques to put your body into a state of total relaxation.* Relaxation exercises have a natural tranquilizing effect that can induce sleep. The techniques discussed in a later chapter will help condition the brain to instruct the rest of the body to achieve a deeply relaxed state. Once there, we'll be able to fall asleep quite easily.

We don't realize how necessary sleep is until we don't get enough of it. Lack of sleep tends to be cumulative and can lead to increased problems with resistance and susceptibility to illness, but by developing proper sleep patterns, we gain the dual advantage of feeling better and staying healthier.

DIET, STRESS AND DEPRESSION

You are what you eat, the expression goes. Is there a link between what we eat and how we feel? Research being done at medical centers around the country does in fact indicate that some cases of depression may be triggered by nutrition and diet. Studies have also shown that stress, fatigue and anxiety can prevent vitamin and mineral absorption and disrupt nutrient pathways that manufacture important brain chemicals like serotonin (5-HT), noradrenaline, melatonin and tryptophan. This is why it's especially important to maintain a balanced diet and take vitamin and mineral supplements during times of stress.

Both serotonin and noradrenaline, derived from amino acids founds in meats, dairy products and other food supplements, act as neurotransmitters, which send messages from the brain to the rest of the body. When these transmitters are blocked or interfered with, our normal brain and bodily functions are impaired. Low levels of serotonin cause aggression, irritability, suicidal behavior, insomnia, depression and disrupted biorhythms.

In both human and animal studies, subjects with the lowest serotonin levels tend to exhibit the most aggressive or violent behavior. Furthermore, research has shown that serotonin-lowering drugs increase aggression while serotonin-stimulating drugs lessen anger and aggressive behavior. Medications such as Prozac, which boost serotonin, work because they reduce the biochemical reactions associated with stress. Psychiatrists who have studied the buffering effects of brain serotonin on behavior have dubbed it the "stress immunizer."

The dietary amino acid, tryptophan, is converted to serotonin and eventually to melatonin, which helps us maintain internal biological rhythms. Because it inhibits the sympathetic nervous system, which stimulates heart rate, breathing and blood flow, melatonin is considered an important anti-stress hormone. Low levels of melatonin have been associated with depression, premenstrual syndrome, alcoholism, decreased immunity and aging.

The relationship between stress, depression and serotonin is important, because one of the vital functions of serotonin is to induce drowsiness and sleep. Sleep, in turn, is an effective mechanism for helping us relax and for relieving symptoms of depression. In some cases, insomnia only prolongs the amount of time spent dwelling on problems.

Though we're only now beginning to understand the complex mechanisms of sleep, we do know that prolonged periods of sleep deprivation can cause irritable and sometimes neurotic behavior. It also makes us more susceptible to stress and stress reactions. Sleep, therefore, brings us back to a state of balance and makes us more resistant to the effects of stress. By increasing our tryptophan intake, which affects serotonin levels, we may be able to avoid the onset of depression.

Depression caused by low noradrenaline levels may be avoided by increasing our intake of the amino acid phenylalanine, which is converted by the body to tyrosine, the building block of noradrenaline. Phenylalanine supplements, however, should not be taken without the advice of a physician since they may have adverse side effects in people with hypertension. So, as more is learned about the effects of what we eat, we can say for certain that food affects the mind, which in turn can trigger changes in virtually every part of our body.

The best serotonin boosters are foods such as whole grains, barley, brown rice, carrots, celery, corn, oatmeal, onions, potatoes, radishes, squash, turnips and yams. Animal products like turkey, for example, that contain the amino acid tryptophan, which is then converted to serotonin, are also good. A word of caution, however: proteins have a tendency to compete with carbohydrates for entry into the brain and therefore, it's best to alternate high-protein meals with high carbohydrate meals. But the best way to lift your mood by raising serotonin levels is to moderate proteins and make sure that every meal contains complex carbohydrates, especially whole grains, fruits and vegetables.

ANTIDEPRESSANTS AND
STRESS REACTIONS

Since ancient times, healers have put their faith in just about anything to cure mental illness. Potions, mineral baths, crushed herbs, vapors and bromides have all been used. The successful breakthroughs, though, came in the 1950s with the development of antidepressants and tranquilizers. Since then, the prescription of antidepressant drugs has become a multi-billion dollar business, with more than fifty million prescriptions for such drugs filled in any given year.

With all the success, however, comes a dark side. Antidepressant drugs can actually lead to more serious illness and disease because they often cause severe stress reactions. This occurs for two reasons. Since depression is such a complicated disorder, affecting individuals in many different ways, certain antidepressants can have side effects which create anxiety and physical disability. Individuals taking antidepressants should be cognizant of symptoms and need to consult their physicians as soon as they become aware of physical or emotional changes. Because some antidepressants need to be taken for as long as six weeks before they begin to work, depressed individuals may become discouraged or impatient and stop taking the drugs. This can cause further depression and stress because they feel as if nothing can help.

Most antidepressant drugs fall into four major classes: tricyclic drugs, MAO inhibitors, lithium and selective serotonin reuptake inhibitors (SSRIs). A fifth type, which is unrelated to the others, is Wellbutrin (bupropion). When someone begins to take antidepressants, improvement is usually not immediate. It often takes several weeks and sometimes months, before noticeable changes occur and even then some symptoms will diminish early on while others take longer. If little or no change is evident, then a different medication may be warranted. Since some people respond better to one type of medicine than another, a physician may have to keep changing prescriptions until one is found that works.

Although they can work wonders, each antidepressant drug has certain side effects and may cause unique emotional distress by interfering with normal bodily functions. This, of course, can lead to negative physical reactions. Sometimes the drug interacts with another drug or a food item. When antidepressants cause unexpected side effects, they invariably trigger spontaneous stress reactions, which further aggravate the depression. In many cases, changing the drug or the dosage or avoiding certain medications or foods can relieve symptoms.

MUTUAL HELP GROUPS

For many of our problems, there are no easy answers or simple cures, but there are alternatives to coping alone. Mutual help groups can aid us in finding the hope and personal support we need because they offer us the most important outlet for recovery—the understanding and help of others who have gone through similar experiences.

Mutual help has been practiced since families first existed. As social beings, all of us need to be accepted, cared for and emotionally supported. We also find it very satisfying to care for and support those around us. Within the most natural mutual help networks—our families and friends—we establish the one-to-one contact so important to our happiness and well-being. This informal support is such a basic part of our social character that we're apt to take it for granted, but it clearly influences our ability to handle distressing events in our lives. Many of our daily conversations are actually mutual counseling sessions whereby we exchange the reassurances and advice that help us deal with routine stresses. In fact, research scientists have found that there's a strong link between the strength of our social support systems and our health.

The personal support we receive from family and friends, however, is only one part of the support network that helps sustain us through life. As we develop socially and intellectually, we tend to associate with others who have similar interests and beliefs. In groups such as religious congregations, civic and fraternal organizations and social clubs, members benefit from a shared identity and a sense of common purpose. Through combined efforts, these groups often can promote or accomplish what the individual, acting alone, cannot. Our reasons for joining groups may vary considerably, but each member's presence and participation adds to the strength of the group. Thus, the group becomes an instrument for service to the total membership.

There are a number of ways to get information about mutual help groups. Some of the larger ones are listed by subject in the phone directory and the names and phone numbers of many more are available from hospitals and local mental health and social-service agencies. Directories of mutual help groups usually can be found in public libraries. As an introduction, I've listed some of the more common mutual help groups in the back of the book.

Throughout this chapter, one coping strategy stands out more than any other and that is the idea of developing social support systems and becoming involved with other people. No other stress therapy has had so much impact on so many different emotional problems. As a society-oriented people, we need other people to relate to and to communicate with. Without this part of our existence, most of us would be unable to deal with the mounting stresses that we're constantly subjected to at work and at home.

We can't be individual islands and expect to survive emotionally in a society that places such a premium on social support. When we deny ourselves the opportunity to interrelate with others, we're diminished, because we don't allow ourselves to be involved with humankind. We're all part of society in general and our community in particular. Unless we take advantage of our strong human need to have relationships with other people and become involved with one another, we'll continue to have high rates of stress-induced adult and childhood disease, mental health problems and suicide. In our stress-filled society, we all have a stake in each other's lives.

Chapter 7

Childhood and
Adolescent Stress

Adults don't have a monopoly on stress. In fact, as many will remember, childhood can be a time of tremendous anxiety and emotional upheaval. The reason children seem less stressed than adults is that they're normally more resilient and less likely to succumb to illnesses and diseases caused by stress reactions. Rather than exhibiting physical symptoms (even though physical symptoms do occur), children usually respond to stress with overt emotional and behavioral problems. These problems may be a strong indicator that your child is experiencing some sort of stress in his or her life. The following is a list of the most common life change events typically experienced by children and which can be serious sources of stress:

STRESSFUL LIFE EVENTS
FOR CHILDREN

I. EVENTS EXPERIENCED BY PARENTS
Death of a parent
Separation of parents
A parent who is an alcoholic or abuses drugs
Parent out of work who is usually employed
Marital reconciliation for separated parents
A divorced parent begins to date or remarries
Parent in jail or prison
A parent remains depressed for an extended time period

II. EVENTS EXPERIENCED BY THE FAMILY
Death of a sibling or extended family member
Prolonged separation from parent

Severe illness of a family member
Birth of a sibling
The addition of a new person to the household
A sibling leaves home
Death of a pet
Change of residence
Lack of supervision for prolonged periods
Family financial problems
Vacation with the family

II. EVENTS EXPERIENCED BY THE CHILD

Serious physical illness, injury or hospitalization
Sexual abuse or exploitation by an older person
Physical abuse, including harsh physical punishment
Emotional abuse
Physical abnormality or deformity
Beginning or ending school
Being retained or accelerated a grade in school
A change in recreation—starting a new sport in school
Outstanding personal achievement
Change in eating habits
Being picked last by a team or group
Going to the dentist or doctor
Starting physical changes or puberty
Starting to date
Toilet training
Difficulty making and keeping friends

Many life changes experienced by children involve problems within the family such as divorce, illness or death. Therefore, a child who doesn't necessarily experience personal stress directly still may be stressed as a result of his or her parents' stress. As parents, we need to be aware of how even small life changes or personal problems can affect our children, who are keenly in tune with everything that's going on in their home environments.

Just as adults experience stress symptoms, children under stress will exhibit certain symptoms that manifest themselves as behavior or personality problems. You should watch for key symptoms such as excessive crying, withdrawal, aggression or regression. Other key symptoms to be particularly aware of are:

I. PHYSICAL SYMPTOMS

Sleep problems such as insomnia, sleepwalking or excessive sleep

Eating or weight problems
Excessive crying with no provocation
Teeth grinding—asleep or awake
Clumsiness or accident proneness
Listlessness or fatigue
Nervous tics such as muscle twitching, nail biting, eye blinking, etc.
Bed-wetting (especially older children)
Nightmares
Stuttering or stammering
Difficulty concentrating or easily distracted

II. BEHAVIORAL SYMPTOMS
Regression to younger behaviors
Failure in school
Cruelty to animals or people
Stealing
Running away
Destroying things
Lying or cheating
Temper tantrums
Excessive daydreaming
Perfectionistic—must have everything exactly right
Drug abuse

II. RELATIONAL AND SELF-ESTEEM SYMPTOMS
Withdrawal or unwillingness to try
Feelings of hopelessness
Referring to oneself as dumb, stupid or incapable
Making suicidal statements like "I want to die" or "I wish I never
     was born"
Excessive fears
Loss of friends
Other children avoid or act as if he/she were weird
Does not join in group activities

TALKING ABOUT TERRORISM

Since 9/11, children in America have been more aware of the threat of terrorism than we realize. Sadly, in some countries children face threats of terrorism daily. No matter how hard we try to protect them, we can't prevent them from watching television or listening to the radio and hearing something about a potential bombing or an attack on civilian targets. In addition to what they learn from the media, children take emotional cues from the adults in their lives who are also concerned about safety. Here are some ways to address the needs of our children in the aftermath of violence or terrorist attacks:

- *Create a calm and relaxed environment through your own demeanor.* If your children are visibly anxious or upset, take time to explain your own feelings and why.

- *Take the time to listen and answer questions.* Ask your children what they know and what's bothering them. Many children are curious about the images they see on television. Don't ignore your child's need to learn about what's going on in the world.

- *Reinforce to your children that you are doing everything to ensure that they are safe.* Assure them that adults are working to make their homes and schools as safe as possible.

- *Help your children separate fact from fiction.* By answering questions honestly, you will counter the speculation and exaggerations they may be hearing on TV or from their friends.

- *Make an effort to limit your children's television, radio and internet activity in order to avoid excessive exposure to violent imagery.* Consider activities in which you and your children can engage instead.

- *If your family has a strong faith, talk to your children about that faith and help them relate what has happened to those beliefs.* Help them understand the presence of good and evil in the world. This is also a good time to pray for individuals who have been touched by the destruction and loss of life.

- *If your children are very upset, it's okay to change routine behaviors for a short while.* Allowing them to sleep with you, for example, will reassure them, although you need to create a clear understanding that the routine is only temporary.

- *Engage your children in activities where they can offer constructive assistance to the victims of violence.* With young children, you may help him or her send drawings and cards to victims or first responders like firefighters and police officers. If your child is older, he or she may want to donate blood or volunteer with a community organization that is offering help to victims of terrorist attacks.

WARNING SIGNS OF CHILDHOOD STRESS

We spend so much time with our children that it's not always easy to recognize when they're stressed out. Little things are often over-looked. Behaviors are chalked-up to changes that normally occur as they grow up. Dreams are attributed to something they may have watched on television or in a movie. Mood swings, physical ailments and emotional outbursts are taken as signs that "kids are just being kids." What we often miss in the heat of day-to-day conflicts and inter-actions are the visible clues and warning signals telling us that some-thing different is going on and that our kids simply are not coping.

Evidence based on MRIs and PET scans shows that the wiring within young brains (i.e. nerve connections) continue to sprout, develop and grow during childhood and well into adolescence. What this tells us is that kids' brains are not yet mature enough to handle life stresses the way we expect them to. As a result, young people exhibit reckless behavior, they have a difficult time organizing and planning, they have different biorhythms and sleep patterns than the rest of us and they become impulsive and irresponsible. In short, they're responding to stress and to their environment in the only way their brains will allow. These responses can be even more dramatic during the preteen and teenage years, when parents suddenly discover that their youngster has been transformed from a sweet, lovable child into a moody and disobedient teen.

All children experience stress symptoms at one time or another. But if the symptoms persist, or if there are multiple symptoms that continue to reoccur, you need to take a closer look at what it is that's causing the stress in your child's life. Sometimes only a professional can identify and assess the reasons or causes and even prescribe med-ication for more serious problems. In most cases, stress is easy to cope with if we know what it is we're dealing with in the first place. Our job as parents, teachers, counselors and coaches is to first recognize symptoms of stress common at various age levels and then use spe-cific techniques to help children of any age get through those stress-ful moments in their lives.

WARNING SIGNS, AGES 6-10

The younger a child is, the more difficult it is for him/her to communicate problems and the more likely that stress will be exhibited as a behavioral response. Children this age react, sometimes violently, in frustration or because of their inability to explain what's wrong. Little things, insignificant to older children, may be traumatic for a six- or seven-year old. Changes in daily routines such as bedtimes, school, babysitters, or parents taking on new jobs, can trigger anxiety in young children that can lead to physical and emotional problems.

Parents and teachers need to be on the lookout for sudden physical and behavioral changes specific to this age group. Things to look for are:

- New or recurrent bedwetting
- Disrupted sleep patterns, especially getting up in the middle of the night with nightmares
- Persistent change in eating habits
- Regressive behavior such as thumb sucking, uncontrollable crying, hair pulling or clinging to parents, if these behaviors have not been typical
- Sudden onset of nausea, vomiting or stomach pains
- Marked change of interest in things the child has previously enjoyed
- Sudden fears about going to school, riding a bus, playing with friends, the weather, etc.

Young children whose parents instill in them a good sense of self-esteem, encourage them when they encounter difficulties and teach them how to communicate and solve problems, cope much better with stress. At this age, observation and mimicking are part of life. Children learn to cope from parents; and parents who remain calm, do not outwardly exhibit fear and anxiety and work through stressful situations in a reassuring manner, invariably raise children who will grow up to be good stress managers.

WARNING SIGNS, AGES 10-14

As children mature, reach early adolescence and go through puberty, the way they respond to stress changes with them. Some studies have shown that boys at this age don't cope as well as girls, possibly because society still expects boys to act brave and not show their emotions. As a result, warning signs of stress may not always be obvious with boys.

This could be an especially difficult time of life because of increasingly complex social interactions, the beginnings of peer pressure, the need to fit in and parents' desires to have their children achieve and excel in school, sports, or other activities. The most common warning signs for ten- to fourteen-year-olds are:

- Depression or sudden onset of sadness
- Aggression or bouts of violent behavior
- Marked change in school performance and/or concentration
- Withdrawal and isolation
- Regression to more childlike behaviors like thumb sucking or talking in a babyish manner
- Unwillingness to participate in family or school activities
- Unwillingness to talk or to ask questions, especially if the child has been normally vocal or curious

At this age, children are still open and willing to talk. We should take advantage of that by listening to their complaints and picking up on the distress signals they may be sending. How we help them handle stress during the middle school years will set the stage for those difficult teenage years. The earlier and more effectively our children learn to cope with stress, the easier it will be for them to do so later.

WARNING SIGNS, AGES 14-18

Once those hormones kick in and a child reaches the teenage high school years, an entirely new set of issues come into play. A teen's world is full of dilemmas, mood swings, confusion, anger and frustration over everything from homework to love. There's preoccupation with looks, peer and family relationships and role changes. Sometimes there's no middle ground. It's either emotional feast or famine and parents have to realize that at this most critical stage of life, their children need more understanding and help in coping with stress than at any other time.

Because a teenager's brain is not yet wired to avoid risks, some of the warning signs are related to risk-taking. Kids in this age group react to stress by acting out in specific ways and can, in fact, place themselves or others in danger without even thinking about it. Some of the warning signs to look for are:

- A breakdown in interpersonal relationships
- Isolation and withdrawal, especially when the teen is generally outgoing
- Unwillingness to accept responsibility at home, school or on the job

- Unusual boredom, fatigue and/or loss of interest
- Decreased self-esteem
- Sudden depression and/or irritability
- Sudden onset of physical problems like loss of appetite, increased blood pressure, stomach pains, exhaustion, asthma or skin disorders

It's easy to overlook stress in teenagers, because we assume that what we see as bizarre behavior is part of the physical and emotional changes they're going through. But we need to be aware of events surrounding our children's lives, because they may be giving us a heads up that the behavior is actually stress-related. When asked to list what they considered most stressful, adolescents named the following.

1. A parent dying
2. A brother, sister or close friend dying
3. Divorce or separation
4. Parent, relative or other family member becoming very sick (cancer, for example)
5. Failing one or more subjects in school
6. Parent losing a job
7. Breaking up with a boyfriend or girlfriend

It doesn't take much for a teenager to get stressed out under the best of conditions. Add death, divorce, illness or a broken relationship and you have the ingredients for real problems. As a child moves through these tough years, parents may feel as if they're constantly walking on eggshells. Outbursts and arguments shouldn't keep parents from getting involved just to keep the peace. By separating normal outbursts from cries for help and by identifying stress symptoms right away, especially when their children are experiencing traumatic life events, parents will ensure that stress doesn't get out of hand and lead to more serious physical and emotional disorders.

WARNING SIGNS OF POST-TRAUMATIC STRESS DISORDER (PTSD)

Any frightening or stressful event—physical or sexual abuse, traumatic injury, a natural disaster, incidents like 9/11—can trigger PTSD. Within a few days or weeks, usually after the child has had a chance to think about what happened, uneasy feelings begin to emerge. The child is more nervous than usual, defensive and seems to want to avoid anything that would remind him or her of the event. If these feelings and behaviors last more than a month, the child may be officially diagnosed as having Post Traumatic Stress Disorder.

According to the Department of Health and Human Services, as many as 30 percent of children who experience traumatic events develop PTSD. Many children whose friends or family members were affected by 9/11, for example, shared in the grief and developed PTSD symptoms to some extent. Statistics also show that children who appear to have little initial reaction to an event are less likely to develop PTSD and children who have had previous traumatic experiences, have exhibited strong initial reactions or whose support systems (parents, teachers, etc.) are very distressed by the event, are at much higher risk. The three main categories of warning signs are:

- **Re-experiencing the trauma**. Sudden thoughts or feelings about the traumatic event may suddenly pop into the child's mind. Nightmares or flashbacks are common, as are crying spells, increased heart rate or other physical symptoms like sweating or stomach pains when reminded of the event.

- **Avoiding Reminders of the Trauma**. Children tend to avoid or try to avoid people, places or activities that will remind them of what happened. Sometimes a child will become detached or emotionally numb in order to avoid the painful feelings and emotions associated with the event. If allowed to go on too long, the detachment can intensify and lead to withdrawal from friends and a feeling of hopelessness about the future.

- **Hyper-arousal**. A common response following trauma is to become overly excited, jumpy and hypersensitive to loud noises and sudden movements. A child may become guarded and on the lookout for signs of danger, be irritable and angry or have trouble sleeping or concentrating.

Reactions to traumatic events often vary according to age. Some children are more vulnerable than others and their reactions may be more intense or long lasting. Here are some differences between children of different ages according to the National Institute of Mental Health:

Children five years of age and younger: Typical reactions can include fear of being separated from parents, crying, whimpering, screaming, immobility and/or aimless motion, trembling, frightened facial expressions and excessive clinging. Parents may also notice children returning to behaviors exhibited at earlier ages (regressive behavior), such as thumb sucking, bedwetting and fear of the dark. Children this young tend to be strongly affected by their parents' reaction to the traumatic event.

Children six to eleven years old: School age children may show extreme withdrawal, disruptive behavior and/or an inability to concentrate or pay attention. Also common are regressive behaviors, nightmares, sleep problems, irrational fears, irritability, refusal to attend school, outbursts of anger and fighting. Physical symptoms include stomachaches, nausea and vomiting, or other ailments with unknown causes. Because children may become depressed, schoolwork often suffers as well.

Adolescents twelve to seventeen years old: Older children may exhibit responses similar to adults, including flashbacks, nightmares, emotional numbing, avoidance of any reminders of the traumatic event, depression, substance abuse, problems with peers and antisocial behavior. Adolescents often go into periods of withdrawal and isolation, develop physical ailments and sleep problems, have thoughts of suicide and go into academic decline. This is an age group that tends to confide more in friends than in family and, therefore, parents need to know who their children's friends are. Sometimes it's easier to get information out of your child's friends than from your own child.

It's important to distinguish simple stress from PTSD, which lasts much longer and might lead to behaviors that can endanger the child or others. Adults need to be on the lookout for chronic behavioral changes following a traumatic event and then: (1) speak with the child openly about it; (2) listen to the child as he/she expresses feelings and emotions; (3) help the child cope with the fear and anxiety associated with the trauma by focusing on his/her strengths and talents; and (4) seek professional help and counseling if necessary. Getting help from a mental health professional with experience in childhood trauma is often critical in stemming more serious emotional health issues.

CHILDREN AND DEPRESSION

Even happy children become depressed at one time or another and like adults may exhibit different signs and symptoms of their depression. Depending on whether the problem is stress-related or something more serious, childhood depression can be as simple as feeling

sad or as severe as deep withdrawal, in which the child becomes isolated and finds it impossible to function normally.

Depression that goes on for weeks or months is called clinical
depression, which is far more serious than the ordinary "down moods"
all children experience now and then and which pass after a visit with
a friend or a good movie. Clinical depression, at times triggered for no
apparent reason, is a whole body disorder affecting the way we think
and feel both physically and emotionally. It should always be taken
seriously, since it can deepen and lead to thoughts of suicide or to violent behavior.

The good news is that nearly eighty percent of people with clinical
depression, including children, are treated successfully with medications, psychotherapy or a combination of both. Even the most serious
cases usually respond to the right therapy. The most common causes
of stress-induced depression are life changes (negative as well as positive), traumatic events, distorted perceptions and, in the case of older
children, high expectations and life demands.

Among both children and adolescents, depression is often misdi-
agnosed as normal mood swings associated with development, common anxiety or social problems. Therefore, we need to make sure that
we're not mistaking a chemical imbalance that affects millions of children under the age of eighteen with a simple stress disorder. Not recognizing and treating depression early can have far reaching effects,
leading to physical illness, substance abuse and suicidal behavior. If
five or more of the following symptoms persist for two or more weeks,
it may indicate major depression rather than a stress response:

- Frequent vague, non-specific physical complaints such as
  headaches, muscle aches, stomach pains or fatigue
- Persistent sad or irritable mood
- Loss of interest in activities once enjoyed
- Difficulty sleeping or oversleeping
- Feelings of worthlessness or hopelessness
- Difficulty concentrating
- Frequent absences from school or poor performance in
  school
- Talk of or efforts to run away from home
- Outbursts of shouting, complaining, unexplained irritability
  or crying
- Being bored
- Lack of interest in being with friends
- Alcohol or substance abuse
- Social isolation, poor communication

- Fear of death
- Extreme sensitivity to rejection or failure
- Increased irritability, anger or hostility
- Reckless behavior
- Difficulty with relationships

In childhood, boys and girls are equally at risk for depression. During adolescence, however, girls are twice as likely as boys to develop depressive disorders. This is especially true if there's a family history of the disorder, particularly if one of the parents experienced depression at an early age rather than later in life. The greatest risk factors, according to the National Institute of Mental Health, include:

- Stress
- Cigarette smoking
- Loss of a parent or loved one
- Break up of a romantic relationship
- Attention, conduct or learning disorders
- Chronic illness, such as diabetes
- Abuse or neglect
- Other trauma, including natural disasters

BIPOLAR DISORDER

Also known as manic-depression, bipolar disorder is less common in children than it is in adults. And as happens with depression, symptoms may be mistaken for normal emotions and behaviors that are typical of that age group. Unlike normal and temporary mood changes, bipolar disorder significantly impairs a child's ability to function in school, at home with the family, or with friends. Statistics show that 20 to 40 percent of adolescents with major depression develop bipolar disorder within five years after the onset of their depression.

The main characteristic of bipolar disorder is an extreme and/or rapid shift in behavior from episodes of depression to episodes of unusually high energy. An individual may be sad and irritable, then giddy and elated; energetic, hyperactive and attentive, then suddenly exhausted; have thoughts of worthlessness and even suicide, followed by thoughts of worth, self-esteem and even grandiosity. Other manifestations may include alcohol or substance abuse and difficulty in maintaining relationships.

When bipolar disorder begins before the onset of puberty, it is often characterized by a continuous, rapid-cycle, irritable and mixed symptom state that may coexist with disruptive behavior disorders, particularly attention deficit hyperactivity disorder (ADHD) or conduct disorder (CD). In contrast, later adolescent or adult-onset bipolar disorder tends to occur suddenly, often with a classic manic episode and to have a more episodic pattern with relatively stable periods. There's also less co-occurring ADHD or CD among those who develop the disorder later.

Existing evidence indicates that bipolar disorder beginning in childhood may be a more severe form of the illness than older adolescent and adult-onset bipolar disorder. Any child or adolescent who appears depressed and/or exhibits ADHD-like symptoms that are very severe, with outbursts and mood changes, should be evaluated by a psychiatrist or psychologist with experience in bipolar disorder. This is especially critical if there's a family history of the illness. The evaluation is important because psychostimulant medications for ADHD may actually worsen manic symptoms.

Treatment of both depression and bipolar disorder in children and adolescents involves psychotherapy, medication or a combination of both and targeted interventions involving the home or school environment. It's important for parents to understand these illnesses and the treatments that may be prescribed since side effects and interactions can occur. In many cases, early intervention and proper treatment helps children and adolescents make full and lasting recoveries.

DEALING WITH ANGER

Anger, along with joy, sadness and curiosity, is one of the four basic emotions experienced by children. It's as natural to be angry as it is to be happy. But the news these days about angry and violent children is startling. Increasingly, single parent families, poverty, abuse and social stresses are causing our children to feel more and more alienated. Intense anger is an emotion that often emerges as a result of frustration. Frustration then leads to rage and rage can lead to deadly consequences, because the young person may feel as if there is no other way out.

Childhood anger, besides having a psychological impact, has a physical impact as well. According to a recent study published in the Journal of the American Medical Association, young adults who scored high on tests designed to measure anger and hostility were already in the process of developing heart disease well before showing physical symptoms. The study, which followed 374 individuals over a 10-year period, found that those with the highest hostility scores a decade earlier had the greatest amount of plaque buildup in their coronary arteries. This was the first study to show a link between a physical disorder such as heart disease and emotions such as anger in young people.

The implications are obvious. Since the mind-body connection in young people is already at work, parents and teachers need to get involved in teaching children anger management techniques as early as possible in order to prevent future illness and disease. The problem children have is that they often react to situations without thinking first. Here are some suggestions to help your child develop coping skills and deal with his or her anger.

- **Reinforce good behavior.** Too often we react negatively to bad behavior, but fail to acknowledge when a child deals with his or her anger in a positive way. Here's where conditioning and habit formation come into play. By reinforcing the child's good behavior with encouraging words and rewards, you are helping to condition your child's developing brain in a way that will help control anger and alter bad behavior.

- **Set a good example.** Evaluate your own responses to life events and make sure you are acting in a way that you would like your child to act. Ask yourself the question, "Is this how I would want my child to act?" If it's not, then your child may be learning negative behavior patterns by imitating you.

- **Listen to your child's feelings.** Pay particular attention to how he or she is dealing with problems in school or relationships. In many cases, anger is simply an outward expression of failure, rejection or frustration. Since young people are not able to deal effectively with complex situations, it's important that you get clues about their problems from the things they say and how they feel about them.

- **Make sure your child knows how to address and solve problems.** Children's brains are not yet ready to cope with the same stresses as adults' brains are and they often feel helpless in their inability to solve problems. It's not surprising, then, that anger is often their first response. Children who are taught to think about the consequences of their actions and ways to deal with issues are less likely to lash out in frustration.

- **Provide a comforting and secure environment in which your child is free to express emotions.** Anger is often triggered when there's a sense that nothing matters and there's nowhere to go to vent feelings. Providing an environment in which the child can freely discuss and even argue, without fear of reprisal is vital if you want to keep the lines of communication and dialogue open.

Day-to-day problems and frustrations that to us seem trivial can be significant for children and adolescents. They simply can't deal with many life issues because their brain wiring is not quite finished. The result is anger, violence or worse. If you're unsuccessful in helping your child cope with angry feelings, no matter what you do or how hard you try, don't hesitate to seek professional help. There may be a more serious underlying problem. Anger, according to experts, is a symptom of many childhood medical conditions, including ADHD, bipolar disorder and depression.

A good child psychologist is invaluable in testing for learning disabilities that may be the real source of anger and also in recognizing symptoms of hidden emotional and mental disorders that are often treated successfully through medication and/or behavior modification. A child's brain, though not quite developed, is more complex than we once had realized. By working things out together, the child and parent will build a relationship that is stronger and less likely to result in bouts of anger and violence.

Even though the brain is not fully developed in children and adolescents, the mind-body connection is still an important component of their overall health and well-being. The mind provides direction to bodily functions such as immunity, but it does so differently when it comes to perceptions and stress-related reactions. Children are not miniature adults; they are unique individuals with a unique set of physiological mechanisms.

Because the young brain is malleable and neural connections are still growing, it's important to remember that how we interact with our children can very well determine how healthy they are, both physically and mentally, for the rest of their lives. We need to be aware of stages of child development so that we don't expect too much or too little from them. We should help our children set realistic goals based on their talents and limitations, then help them achieve their potential. We must love them unconditionally and teach them to love as well as respect others. And we should discipline fairly and consistently, but always allow them to express their thoughts and feelings so that they remain open to communication. Caring for a young mind early on will guarantee a healthy body and a powerful mind-body connection throughout life.

:60 SECOND STRESS
MANAGEMENTS
FOR CHILDREN

All normal children have some stress symptoms at one time or another, but if your child exhibits several of these symptoms simultaneously or for prolonged periods of time, you may need to take a closer look at what it is that's causing these symptoms. Sometimes a professional is needed to identify and assess the reasons or causes for stress and to prescribe specific stress management techniques designed for children. But as a parent, you may want to try the following nine strategies in order to help your children better manage their stress:

1. *Moderate your children's activities.* Never allow children to take on too many activities at the same time. Whether they're involved in sports, academics or work, children need to pace themselves just like adults in order to prevent burnout and keep from developing stress symptoms. But unlike adults, children aren't as able to manage their time efficiently and can't cope with activity overload. Moderating their activities will help your children maintain a more balanced and stress-free lifestyle.

2. *Show your children physical affection.* One of our more basic human attributes is our need to be touched, hugged and kissed. Children especially need to be held during times of stress so that they feel reassured and safe. Telling your children how you feel and how much you love them also will soothe their stress and at the same time teach them to verbally communicate their feelings with others.

3. *Teach your children proper assertiveness.* Your children need to know how to deal properly with angry feelings, how to cope with criticism, how to say no and how to stand up for themselves. By expressing themselves verbally, children also will feel more in control and thus reduce their need to act out negative behavior

4. *Give your children the attention they deserve.* All children naturally thrive on attention. So make certain that your children are praised regularly and listened to. Whenever children sense they're being ignored, they begin to exhibit undesirable behaviors in order to get attention. Paying attention to your children is one

of the best ways to assure them that you really care about what they're doing and how they're feeling.

5. *Set reasonable goals.* In order to prevent the stress of failure, don't expect perfection from your children. Whenever you expect too much from anyone, you automatically set them up for potential failure and make them feel that what they do is never good enough. So, instead of criticizing small failures, tell your children how much you appreciate their efforts and accomplishments. This praise will perpetuate success, because your children will naturally want to be praised again and again.

6. *Be a role model.* Actions truly speak louder than words. If you deal with anger appropriately, chances are your children will also. If you show affection, share and cooperate with others and communicate feelings properly, your children will as well. Research has even shown, for example, that the values you set for your own health such as drinking, smoking, diet and exercise will leave a lasting impression on your children and instill in them similar values. Therefore, never underestimate the power you have as a positive role model and the influence you wield in molding your children's behavior.

7. *Ease tension through humor.* Humor is a great stress reliever and is one of the best ways to break tension and anxiety. Maintaining a good sense of humor also will teach your children to develop their own senses of humor and, consequently, will give them tools they can use to manage their own stress as adults.

8. *Encourage independent thinking.* As adults, one of the reasons we become stressed is our inability to work out solutions to problems. More than likely this inability is the result of our not being allowed to do things in our own way and to solve problems independently as children. So, instead of trying to work out everything for your children, encourage them to spend time thinking about their problems independently and working through them until they reach solutions. This doesn't mean you shouldn't be there for assistance and support, just that you should really make an effort to help your children think for themselves and learn to come up with intelligent answers.

9. *Spend quiet time with your children.* Spending quiet time with your children will not only help them wind down after a busy day, it also will teach them how to relax. As parents, it's important to be an example to your children so that they grow up having a good sense of how to cope with the stress and anxiety in their lives.

:60 SECOND STRESS MANAGEMENTS FOR HELPING CHILDREN COPE WITH SCHOOL

The first day of school is a milestone in your child's life. It also can be a very traumatic and stressful time of life. Your understanding at this "turning point" is important to the child's future attitude toward school and to his or her healthy growth and development. Experts in child mental health and development emphasize that you, the parent, can play an important role in starting your child off with the self-confidence needed throughout life. This self-confidence is built upon good feelings about parents, about authority figures at school, about other children and about himself or herself as a worthwhile human being.

To help your child cope with school, especially during the early stages when he or she is just beginning, here are some suggestions that can ease the transition from the home environment and make school less stressful from the start.

1. *Make the first day of school an important event.* Starting school is the first major separation from the secure and familiar world of home and family. It marks entrance into a new universe of friendship, learning and adventure. You as parents can never again share completely in this world and, therefore, your greatest gift to your child at this time is your loving support and understanding. Make this day special and exciting.

2. *Prepare your child for the new experience.* Explain to your child what to expect by answering all questions honestly. Children need to know the number of days and the length of time they'll be in school, as well as how to get there and back. A child may be anxious and need to know details in order to handle the stress involved. Working mothers and fathers should make certain that the child knows the arrangements for before and after school care.

3. *Convey a positive attitude about school.* If you as a parent show enthusiasm for what the school experience can mean, your child is more likely to look forward to it.

4. *Make transportation plans clear to your child.* If he or she is to take a bus to school, drive the route together a few times. If there are other children from your neighborhood who are the same age, see if they can drive with you and make it fun. Before your child begins taking the bus, help him or her identify the vehicle. Encourage older children to watch over the younger ones. And once the bus arrives, be direct; say goodbye and allow your child to board alone. If your child cries, try not to overreact; in most cases the tears quickly disappear.

5. *Create a normal, routine atmosphere at home the first few days of school.* Don't deny or avoid the uniqueness of the situation, but do take an active interest in what your child tells you about school when he or she comes home. Be a good listener, allowing time to talk about school and the people there.

6. *Give your child free playtime at home.* Now that your child spends more time in a structured school environment, you need to allow more free time at home for play. Otherwise, your child will begin to associate school with a loss of playtime.

7. *Praise your child for the good things he/she has done.* Remember, there's more to be gained from accentuating the positive. A pat on the back for the right answers can go a long way. Too often we tend to focus on poor performance and behavior.

8. *Treat going to school as part of the normal course of events.* Going to school should be treated as something that's expected of your child and accepted by you. If your child appears nervous about going to school, discuss his or her concern. Show understanding and offer encouragement. A calm, matter-of-fact, positive attitude is your goal. Don't argue the issue of school attendance; it's required by law.

9. *Plan your day so that you can spend time with your child.* Be available when your child needs you. Be sure there's time to talk about school and the happenings of each day.

10. *Avoid comparing your child's experiences with your other chil-*

dren's experiences. Such comparisons can be harmful to a child's self-image. Each of us is different and we meet life's turning points and experiences in our own way.

In rare instances, when a child does not accept school after several days, or when fearfulness and feelings of distress appear and persist, the child may have a problem. At this point, you should seek advice from the school guidance counselor, the teacher, your family physician, school psychologist, community mental health center staff or others who may offer expert advice. But with firm, patient, reassuring handling of your child by you and your child's teacher, your child soon should feel very comfortable away from home and will make new friends quickly. The most important goals for your child during those critical first days of school are to develop feelings of self-confidence and security and to realize that this new part of his or her life is going to be a wonderful and adventurous experience.

:60 SECOND STRESS MANAGEMENTS FOR HELPING CHILDREN COPE WITH GRIEF

Of all the traumatic life experiences a child may face, the death of a parent may be the most traumatic of all. According to Alan Breier of the National Institute of Mental Health, adults who had lost a parent during childhood had a much greater incidence of depression, anxiety and alcoholism that did adults who grew up with healthy parents. These adults were so adversely affected by their loss that the trauma remained with them their entire life. It's important to realize that children before the ages of seven or eight have little or no concept of what death is and, therefore, the sudden loss of someone very close to them can be a profound shock. Some children may be just as deeply affected by the loss of a grandparent, brother, sister or other relative.

When a child experiences the death of a loved one, reactions can vary. Some children become aggressive, angry and hostile, while others become withdrawn and isolated. Other common symptoms to watch for include poor school performance, regressive behavior like bedwetting or thumb sucking and depression. All these behaviors are a way for children to express just how much the death has had an effect on their lives. In order to help a child overcome his or her grief, here are a few strategies you can use to help east the pain and sadness.

1. *Avoid other life changes.* Death is a traumatic enough life expe-

rience for a child. Don't add any more. At this point, the most important thing to do for at least a few months is to make your child feel safe, secure and stable. And that means no unnecessary moving, no family disruptions, no changing schools, no sudden lifestyle shifts and no other major life changes that could make your child feel insecure and unstable.

2. *Express your feelings freely.* Regardless of how much you want to protect your child from pain, he or she needs to feel included in the grieving process. This inclusion makes your child feel like a real part of the family and gives him or her a sense of belonging in every sense of the word. Naturally you don't want to be so emotional that you frighten your child into panic, but at the same time you don't want to exclude your child from what should be an intimately shared experience.

3. *Don't be afraid to talk about death.* Children are inquisitive by nature. They want to ask questions and they need to have answers. In many ways their fantasies about death and dying could be much worse than the reality of death itself. Let your children ask about death and communicate with them in a way that they can understand. Often, questions are a means of reassurance for children. By openly discussing death and answering questions, you'll be lessening their grief and giving them an avenue to vent their feelings and emotions.

:60 SECOND STRESS MANAGEMENTS FOR PRE-TEENS

Your child is in that "in between" age—old enough to understand many adult subjects, yet still young enough to willingly accept guidance from parents. This is a time when you can openly discuss the various stresses of life: peer pressure, alcohol and drug abuse, as well as the relationships your child will have with others. You should take this opportunity to build a special rapport with your child so that communication is there when it is needed.

Stress managements are double-faced during these years. They will enable your child to cope with the pressures he or she will have to face in a very short period of time and they will ease the inherent worries a parent has over a child's ability to cope.

Some :60 second managements are:

1. *Rephrasing a child's comments to show you understand.* This is

sometimes called "reflective listening." Reflective listening serves three purposes: it assures your child you hear what he or she is saying, it allows your child to "rehear" and consider his or her own feelings and it assures you that you correctly understand your child.

2. *Watch your child's face and body language.* Often a child will assure you that he or she doesn't feel sad or dejected, but a quivering chin or too bright eyes will tell you otherwise. When words and body language say two different things, always believe the body language.

3. *Give nonverbal support and encouragement.* This may include a smile, a hug, a wink, a pat on the shoulder, nodding your head, making eye contact, or reaching for your child's hand.

4. *Use the right tone of voice.* Remember that your voice tone communicates to your child as clearly as your words. Make sure your tone doesn't come across as sarcastic or all-knowing.

5. *Use encouraging phrases to show your interest and to keep the conversation going.* Phrases such as "Oh, really?" "Tell me about it." "It sounds as if you..." "Then what happened?" are great for communicating to your pre-teen how much you care. If there's a pause in your conversation, use phrases such as these to encourage your pre-teen to talk.

6. *Give lots of praise.* Look for achievement, even in small tasks and praise your child often. You're more likely to get the behavior you want when you emphasize the positive and your praise will help your child have positive feelings.

7. *Praise effort, not just accomplishment.* Let your child know he or she doesn't always have to win. Trying hard and giving one's best effort is a noble feat in itself.

8. *Help your child set realistic goals.* If the child, or the parent, expects too much, the resulting failure can be a crushing blow. If a pre-teen who is an average athlete announces he plans to become the school quarterback, it might be wise to gently suggest that just making the team would be a wonderful goal and a big honor.

9. *Don't compare your child's efforts with others.* There will always

be other children who are better and worse at a sport than your child, more and less intelligent, more and less artistic, etc. Your pre-teen may not know that a good effort can make you just as proud as a blue ribbon.

10. *When correcting, criticize the action, not the child.* A thoughtless comment can be devastating to a child. A pre-teen still takes an adult's word as law, so parents should know how to phrase corrections.
Helpful Example: "Climbing that fence was dangerous. You could have been hurt, so don't do it again."
Hurtful Example: "You shouldn't have climbed that fence. Don't you have any sense?"

11. *Take responsibility for your own negative feelings.* One constructive way to share you own negative feelings about a situation is to use "I Messages." "I Messages" don't make children feel they are under attack or that they're intrinsically bad.
Helpful Example: "Keeping the house neat is important to me. I get upset when you leave your books and clothes in the hall."
Hurtful Example: "You act like a pig sometimes. When will you learn to put things where they belong?"

12. *Give your child real responsibility.* Children who have regular duties around the house know that they're doing something important to help out. They learn to see themselves as useful and important parts of a team. Completing their duties also instills senses of accomplishment.

13. *Show your children you love them.* Hugs, kisses and saying "I love you" help your children feel good about themselves. Children are never too young or too old to be told that they're loved and highly valued. In families where parents are divorced, it's helpful if the nonresident parent also expresses love and support for the children. When the parent-child relationship is strong and loving, single parent families, including those in which parents are widowed or unmarried, can give their children the same basis for self-esteem as two-parent families.

SIGNS AND SYMPTOMS
OF SUICIDAL BEHAVIOR

Recently, it was discovered that as many as 50 percent of all childhood and adolescent suicides may be disguised to appear as accidents. Since 1960, suicides of young people between the ages of fifteen and twenty-four have gone up nearly 300 percent! Five thousand adolescents die each year from suicide, but the frightening reality is that another 50,000 to 100,000 will attempt suicide unsuccessfully. The only reason why suicide remains the number two cause of adolescent deaths is that it's impossible to prove fatal car accidents (the number one cause of adolescent death) are a means of committing suicide.

In many of these suicide cases, depression was found to be the main component that triggered the suicide in the first place. Depression in these young people is usually the result of negative life events, most notably a high prevalence of broken homes, divorce, or separation. When suicide prone college students were surveyed, the reasons found for intending suicide were: high levels of severe life stress, hopelessness and high levels of depression. Poor problem solvers exhibiting these symptoms were especially at high risk.

As adults we tend to view adolescence as a period of friction, change and problems. For the teenager, it's a very stressful time of concern about weight problems, acne, menstruation, late or early development, sexual arousal, school pressure, boredom, parental hassles, peer pressures and money problems. It's a time of confused feelings, particularly in relationships with parents. Teenagers fight for independence, yet fear too much freedom; they resent overprotection, but need and want parental attention. Because the adolescent years are such a trying period, we often fail to recognize certain signals that indicate suicidal feelings or thoughts. Many times, these signals are a cry for help. Here are some warning signs to look for.

- Isolation and withdrawal from people, especially close friends

- Sudden or gradual loss of interest in appearance

- Unusual change in grades, school work, tardiness or attendance

- Loss of weight and/or appetite

- Insomnia or excessive sleep

- Self-criticism, low self-esteem, feelings of failure or sense of worthlessness

- Preoccupation with death and/or dying

- Loss of interest in previous activities and involvements

- Sudden accident proneness

- Sudden change in personality, especially involving apathy and depression

- Sudden angry outbursts, irritability and hostility

- Excessive use of alcohol or drugs

- Sudden acts of risky or dangerous behavior like speeding in a car or running across a busy street

- Feelings of hopelessness or helplessness

- Suddenly giving away valuable or prized possessions

- Actual threats or verbal cues about not wanting to live anymore

For parents and teachers, it's a challenge to keep a balanced perspective on the teenager's emotional roller coaster ride. As young people bounce back and forth between childhood and adulthood, alternating irresponsibility with responsibility, parents and teacher often don't know what to expect. For this reason, it's even more important to be on a constant lookout for adolescent stress factors and for emotional and behavioral symptoms that may indicate trouble ahead.

The passage of stress-induced child into teenage suicide victim is especially tragic, because, in many cases, the warning signs of depression and suicide are very evident but often overlooked. It's extremely important for families to realize that lines of communication have to remain open between parent and child. If a young person knows that the home is a place where feelings can be expressed freely and ideas shared and exchanged without criticism, that person will be able to deal with stress and depression in a more positive way. As the results of a questionnaire given to adolescents showed, most chose "talking to a friend" as the single most important act they could do to lessen the threat of suicide. Communication is the key. If we can put stress into words, we can begin to interact with one another and develop a bond that will have a tremendous effect on our ability to cope.

When asked about specific problems with parents, teenagers most often cite "not being listened to" as a major source of frustration and anger. Really listening to and communicating with teenagers is difficult and sometimes can be near impossible. But even though adolescence is a trying period, parents and teenagers must keep tuned in to each other to overcome one of the most difficult times in life.

STRESS AND
ADOLESCENCE

One of the greatest times of stress for families is the onset of the adolescent or teenage years. For many families, these are years of turmoil and strife, a period of transition in which newly developing teenagers are honing their social skills and striving for independence and freedom. In today's complex society, these years can be more turbulent than ever before. The frightening reality of AIDS, drugs and violence add a real dimension to stress that makes being a teenager one of the greatest challenges a young person will face. But as much as the stresses of life affects teenagers, they're not alone in their turmoil. If you're the parent of a teenager, you're equally affected and you need to deal effectively with both your teenager's stress as well as the stress you feel as a result of your teenager's stress.

The first step in bringing some harmony back into your life is to recognize that there are certain ideals and expectations you have for your teenager that by themselves will naturally create stress for you. The reason for this is simply that any lack of control over your newly independent child is going to make you feel uncomfortable. You might feel a sense of helplessness as you watch an individual for whom you've done everything for thirteen years suddenly want to do things alone and often in ways that seem strange and controversial. This lack of control sets the stage for confrontation, intolerance and tremendous distress.

:60 SECOND STRESS
MANAGEMENT
FOR PARENTS

If you're a parent of a teenager, you already know the feelings of helplessness and frustration. But you'll develop a greater tolerance—and, at the same time, create a more stress free home environment—by following some simple stress management do's and don'ts.

DO'S

1. *Do* try to set a good example.
2. *Do* give your undivided attention when your teenager wants to talk to you.
3. *Do* try to listen calmly. Don't start preaching.
4. *Do* develop a courteous tone of voice. Respect brings respect. Try not to overreact.
5. *Do* avoid making judgments. Take an interest in your children's activities.
6. *Do* keep the door open on any subject. Respect the adolescent's desire for individuality and independence.
7. *Do* permit expression of ideas and feelings.
8. *Do* encourage self-worth. Build your teenager's confidence; don't degrade it.
9. *Do* be aware of how you treat other children in the family. Try to be fair.
10. *Do* make an effort to say nice things.
11. *Do* hold family conferences.

DON'TS

1. *Don't* expect your teenager to accept every rule and regulation you set forth.
2. *Don't* feel upset or rejected if your teenager tells you he or she hates you.
3. *Don't* try to be a perfect parent because none exist.
4. *Don't* blame your teenager's attitudes and behaviors on your problems.

:60 SECOND STRESS MANAGEMENTS FOR ADOLESCENTS

What responsibilities do teenagers have in decreasing the stress of adolescence and in bridging the generation gap? The following list of stress managers was formulated with the assistance of young people and adults. Have your child read them, tell him or her they were written with the help of teenagers and then talk about these management tools.

1. The first barrier of communication I must cast aside is the attitude of ignoring anybody over thirty. If I expect people to tune in to me, then I must be willing to talk to them.

2. Our generation wants understanding from our elders. In turn, it's only fair that we try to understand them. They have needs and feelings and reasons for their decisions.

3. I will listen to my parents with an open mind and look at the situation from their point of view. That's the way I would expect them to treat me.

4. I will share more of my feelings with my parents. They may have experienced some of the same problems. I need to give them a chance to help me.

5. I want my parents to express trust and confidence in me, to grant me more freedom and responsibility as I mature. It's necessary, then, that I live up to their confidence. What I do reflects on them and they are held accountable for my actions and behavior.

6. Exercising the right to criticize my family, school, friends or society includes the responsibility to suggest how practical improvements can be made.

7. To promote better communications in my family, I will practice courtesy and consideration for others. I will let my parents know I care about them. They're affected by the pressures and problems of everyday living just as I am.

8. When I have a problem that I feel I can't handle, I won't keep it to myself. I'll be responsible enough to talk it out with my parents and, in turn, they'll treat me with the respect and dignity I deserve.

Parents who have overzealous expectations of their teenaged children and who feel a desire to maintain complete control, are doomed to failure.

Certainly it's appropriate to guide, to set limits, to have ground rules and to expect your teenagers to respect others. But if you want your family life to be less stressful and more even keeled, you need to realize that you can't use the same strategies with your teenagers as you do with your younger children. They think differently, they feel differently, they act differently and they require that you adapt a new attitude toward them. By giving up the idea of maintaining total control, you'll not only feel less anxiety and pressure, you'll also be sending a signal to your teenagers that they are being given room to grow. That in itself will create less stress for your teenagers and as a result even less stress for you.

No parent is perfect. There are times after a busy day at work when even the best parent would rather yell "Shut up!" than say "What I hear you saying is that you don't like what I cooked for dinner . . ." Luckily, children are tougher than we think. But we always need to keep in mind that regardless of age, all children experience the stresses of life and are just as prone to stress reactions as we are. And since they are in our care for only a short period of time, we must ensure that they too are able to cope with their stress before it has a lasting negative effect on their health and well-being.

· Chapter 8 ·

Stress and Aging

No one has been able to determine exactly how our bodies age or why we're genetically programmed to live only a certain amount of time. We do know that, as aging continues, our bodies are less likely to respond to challenges and more likely to be affected by negative events and situations. Aging, besides being a physically stressful process, is a very emotionally stressful time of life.

Older people are likely to experience two kinds of stresses: those that are "normal" to aging and those that are imposed by the environment. The stresses of illness, personal loss, diminished income, retirement and inadequate housing, interact with social stresses, such as age-discrimination and a lack of caring, to produce isolation, loneliness and depression.

One of the greatest psychological stresses for older individuals is knowing that there's no change in their ability to learn and carry out mental tasks. Yet, there is widespread bias against them in society and the workplace. This tremendous emotional distress causes depression, which is the most common mental disorder affecting aging individuals. As we age, we allow our negative perceptions of aging to shape our behavior and attitudes. Successful aging can be accomplished only if we eliminate those negative perceptions and learn to cope with the stresses of age in a positive way.

Take the following quiz and see what level of life satisfaction you experience.

A :60 SECOND LIFE
SATISFACTION QUIZ

	AGREE	DISAGREE
1. As I grow older, things seem better than I thought they would be.	_____	_____
2. I've gotten more of the breaks in life than most people I know.	_____	_____
3. This is the dreariest time of my life.	_____	_____
4. I'm just as happy as when I was younger.	_____	_____
5. My life could be happier than it is now.	_____	_____
6. These are the best years of my life.	_____	_____
7. Most of the things I do are boring or monotonous.	_____	_____
8. I expect some interesting and pleasant things to happen to me in the future.	_____	_____
9. The things I do are as interesting to me as they ever were.	_____	_____
10. I feel old and somewhat tired.	_____	_____
11. I feel my age, but it doesn't bother me.	_____	_____
12. As I look back on my life, I'm fairly well satisfied.	_____	_____
13. I wouldn't change my past life even if I could.	_____	_____

14. Compared to other people my age,
I've made a lot of foolish decisions
in my life.   _____   _____

15. Compared to other people my age,
I make a good appearance.   _____   _____

16. I've made plans for things I'll be
doing a month or a year from now.   _____   _____

17. When I think back over my life,
I didn't get most of the important
things I wanted.   _____   _____

18. Compared to other people, I get
down in the dumps too often.   _____   _____

19. I've gotten pretty much what I
expected out of life.   _____   _____

20. In spite of what people say, for most
of us, things are getting worse, not
better.   _____   _____

21. I think about my age so much that
I can't sleep.   _____   _____

22. I get angry more often that I used to.   _____   _____

23. I have as much pep as I did last year.   _____   _____

24. I see enough of my friends and relatives. _____   _____

25. Many times, I feel that life isn't worth
living.   _____   _____

26. Life is hard much of the time.   _____   _____

27. I'm not afraid of very many things
now that I'm older.   _____   _____

28. As I get older, I feel less useful.   _____   _____

29. Compared to other people my age,   ————   ————
  I keep pretty active.

30. I usually don't feel lonely.   ————   ————

   Score one point for each response that indicates life satisfaction. The appropriate life satisfaction responses for each statement are:

1.	Agree	3.	Disagree
2.	Agree	4.	Agree
5.	Disagree	18.	Disagree
6.	Agree	19.	Agree
7.	Disagree	20.	Disagree
8.	Agree	21.	Disagree
9.	Agree	22.	Disagree
10.	Disagree	23.	Agree
11.	Agree	24.	Agree
12.	Agree	25.	Disagree
13.	Agree	26.	Disagree
14.	Disagree	27.	Agree
15.	Agree	28.	Disagree
16.	Agree	29.	Agree
17.	Disagree	30.	Agree

Scoring Key: 25-30 *High Life Satisfaction:* You're aging very successfully because you don't let age get in the way of enjoying life. You have positive attitudes and a good outlook that keep you young at heart.

         15-24 *Average Life Satisfaction:* You need to work on your attitudes and participate in more activities. There are times in your life when you could become more committed. Make sure that negative attitudes and behaviors don't begin to affect your health and well-being. Try to improve those areas on which you scored low.

         0-14 *Low Life Satisfaction.* You're not aging successfully. You need to begin taking immediate steps to improve your overall mental attitude and start participating in activities.

Your goal should be to join clubs, do volunteer work or do anything else that will add interest to your life. Becoming involved can be the first step in transforming your unsuccessful aging into successful aging.

COPING WITH
MIDLIFE CRISIS

As young adults, we use the phrase "midlife crisis" as a kind of joke, because we don't yet think about middle age as something in our immediate future. When we hit thirty, we look at middle age as inevitable and begin thinking more seriously about how we're going to face that time of life. And by the time we turn forty, we finally realize that we're at the midpoint of our lives and what we thought of as an inevitable but distant event has finally arrived. For many of us, this event can be a very stressful, if not traumatic, period of life.

Men and women differ significantly in how they initially react to the onset of middle age. According to experts, a man often experiences anxiety, feelings of inadequacy and depression over his failure to achieve the goals he set out to accomplish. He may become despondent over his career, which he feels is going nowhere or which he no longer enjoys. He may become even more despondent if he believes that he's too old to do anything else and that he'll spend the rest of his life doing exactly what he's doing. A woman, on the other hand, experiences more happiness and fulfillment. She may be less bored, less lonely and feel much better about herself and her future.

Even though men and women may begin mid-life differently, they both end up discovering greater life satisfaction as they age. By the time they reach fifty or fifty-five, men and women have usually gone through the worst periods of midlife and really start to enjoy their lives once again.

The key to coping with midlife crises and getting through that 40-to fifty-year-old period, is to realize that middle age is not the end of a satisfying and productive life but that it can be the beginning of a wonderfully enjoyable and fruitful time when we can finally begin to do the things we've always been wanting to do. In today's society especially, middle age often is thought of as the time to experience new activities, explore unknown talents and exploit new opportunities. The problem many of us face when we reach midlife is not our physical or mental health, but our inability or unwillingness to look at our middle years as a time to accomplish most anything we want.

There are four :60 second managements for approaching midlife with a new set of attitudes.

1. *Pursue your interests.* Many older people learn to play musical instruments, take classes, begin painting, and pursue new hobbies because they no longer have to worry about establishing themselves in a career. Forget about being over-the-hill and think about what you plan to accomplish in the long years ahead.

2. *Become involved.* Getting involved with politics, social causes, charities, or hospital work will do wonders for your self-esteem, give new meaning to your life and help you through those critical middle years.

3. *Plan for your future.* Instead of visualizing your future as bleak, visualize it as a time of continued opportunities and great possibilities.

4. *Take time out.* Midlife is the time to breathe. You still have half a lifetime to accomplish your goals.

Many of us begin our adult lives not really exploring our other talents and ambitions. We go through life convincing ourselves that we must spend the rest of our lives doing only what we've been trained to do. As a result, we live with that gnawing question of whether or not we could have been more, accomplished more, or contributed more. You don't have to give up what you already have. But you do need to develop your "shadow" side if you ever expect to reach your full potential and feel fully satisfied that you've become all that you could be.

AGING AND THE DISEASE PROCESS

All living organisms undergo "senescence," a process in which cells begin to die and bodily functions deteriorate. Biological aging involves a progressive decline in nerve transmission, metabolism, rate of blood flow, respiratory capacity, resistance to infection and ability to repair DNA. Factors that speed up this cell degeneration are poor diet, toxins, lack of exercise, unhealthy lifestyle and stress. The longer we live, the more likely it is that the mind-body connection will not respond in the manner it should and, therefore, we become more susceptible to negative life events.

Besides being a physically challenging process, aging is a very emotionally stressful time of life. So it's not unusual to experience some kind of mental health problem as we grow older. The aging or aged individual is more prone to mental illness and stress effects due to several factors.

1. As we age, there is a decrease in the immune system's ability to attack foreign bodies. Therefore, stress makes the elderly more susceptible to illness and disease. Being ill more often than ever before can be traumatic in itself and lead to emotional disorders and a breakdown in mind-body reactions.

2. Increased illness and disease, together with the stress of aging, intensifies conditioned stress responses. This negative conditioning has the effect of making the elderly increasingly more prone to stress-related disorders.

3. The cumulative effect of years of stress reactions begins to take its toll. The more stress episodes the body has had to respond to and overcome, the greater the damage will eventually be.

Scientists are getting close to determining exactly how our bodies age and why we're genetically programmed to live only a certain amount of time. We know for certain that as aging continues our bodies are less likely to respond to challenges and more likely to be affected by negative life events and situations. The process of aging, besides being a physically stressful process, is also a very emotionally stressful time of life. And as with children and younger adults, the mind-body connection plays a significant role in older adults as well.

When people reach the age of sixty, the begin to experience stress normal to the aging process in addition to stressors from their day to day life. Aches, pains, illness, disease, divorce, death, prejudice, retirement and loneliness all contribute to the psychological patterns that begin to build. Collectively, these can influence perceptions and anxieties so much that mind-body networks either under or over respond and trigger a rash of physical problems.

Probably the single greatest psychological stress older individuals experience is their belief that they're no longer good enough to do the things they used to do, especially when it comes to mental tasks. They're not the only ones who hold this view; and the widespread bias against them in society and the workplace is obvious. The resulting depression is one of the most common mental health disorders affecting the aging population.

As we age, we allow many negative perceptions of aging to shape our behavior and attitudes. We let others judge our abilities, even when we know that our abilities may actually have improved with age. As a result, our minds get conditioned and our bodies follow suit by becoming more susceptible to illness and disease. Successful aging (staying mentally and physically healthy into old age) can be accomplished only if we eliminate those negative perceptions and learn to cope with the stresses of age in a positive way.

Age researchers believe that one of the reasons for the increase in disease as we get older is the normal age-related shrinkage of the thymus with an accompanying decrease in thymosin, a hormone that stimulates production of white blood cells. As a result, the elderly have a lowered natural antibody population. In fact, one study showed that 90 percent of young individuals had antibodies against three different flu strains whereas only 63 percent of older individuals did.

Diseases and disease rates vary widely among different countries, which indicate that factors such as genetics, diet and environment contribute to mortality. In Sweden, for example, heart attacks account for more than 40 percent of deaths in people sixty-five to seventy-four years old, whereas in Japan it's less than 10 percent.

Different cancers occur at higher rates in certain countries as well. Colon cancer is highest in countries like the United States where the average diet is low in fiber. In some African countries, it's the lowest in the world. Lung cancer rates are high in countries where smoking rates and concentrations of air toxins are greatest and low in nations where the populations don't smoke as much. Cancer in general, however, increases exponentially after the age of forty.

As we age, many of our systems become less adaptable. In other words, homeostasis is not as efficient as it once had been. Calcium is not absorbed into our bones as readily, our kidneys do not filter blood as well, our lungs have a decreased air capacity, hormones are not released at the same levels and our hearts don't pump with the same strength. We become less tolerant of changes in both external and internal environment, which is the reason most older people just don't adjust well to things like rapid shifts in temperature or blood pressure. Add to this an increase in the amount of stress we expose ourselves to and we have the ingredients for disease.

The reason stress is particularly harmful in old age is that it can lower an already low level of NK and white blood cells. Steady decreases in thymic hormones and reduced lymphocytes and antibodies are further lowered when cortisol is released during stress reactions. The elderly typically don't recover as quickly from infections as younger individuals, but even less so when stressed. Furthermore, HIV-infected patients older than sixty experience significantly shorter amounts of time between their initial infection and full blown AIDS.

Stress, according to some researchers, may also contribute to the onset and progression of Alzheimer's disease. Autopsies performed on Alzheimer's victims show that an important area of the brain involved in learning and memory, the hippocampus, is nearly always damaged. One of the hormones now known to cause that damage is cortisol.

According to Dr. Bruce McEwen of Rockefeller University, hippocampal cells gradually atrophy as part of the normal aging process. The bad news is that cortisol levels during aging are elevated in individuals with hippocampal atrophy and memory impairments associated with that brain region. Chronic stress, therefore, especially during aging, may speed up irreversible loss of hippocampal cells and eventually lead to dementia.

No one has yet determined the genetic causes of aging. All we know is that at some point cells begin to break down both structurally and functionally. We lose our capacity to recover from infections and other invasions and we gradually lose our normal capacity to maintain body functions. Some researchers have shown that while cells may be genetically programmed to self-destruct at a certain time of life, we can postpone the inevitable a bit longer, or at least reduce the most common effects of aging, by improving diet, increasing cardiovascular exercise and reducing stress.

Aging itself can trigger various disease mechanisms, because it is such a physically and emotionally stressful process. Like a vicious cycle, aging increases the likelihood of health problems that, in turn, cause stress that leads to even further health problems. The more stress the elderly experience, the greater the probability that the stress will trigger an even wider variety of illnesses and diseases.

Despite our natural tendency to develop some kind of disease as we age, life expectancy has been rising steadily. As a group, we are taking steps to slow down the aging process by decreasing lifetime exposures to toxins like smoke, radiation and chemicals. We are also more conscious of avoiding physical and emotional stress, eating better and practicing behaviors that will keep our immune systems healthier longer.

There's not much we can do to stop the programmed end of life. And no matter what a few so-called experts say or what some books claim, there is no way that we yet know to reverse aging. What we can do is make sure that life ends naturally and not with a disease that could have been avoided.

GENES AND HUMAN LIFESPAN

During the past century, both life expectancy and the number of individuals sixty-five years of age and older have been increasing steadily. As a result, older people are playing a greater role in government, economics, cultural and social activities, as well as in the work force. And with evidence mounting that older workers can be just as efficient and productive as their younger counterparts, it's not unusual to see companies changing their hiring and retirement practices.

So how far can we keep going before we finally wear out? And is it possible to extend a lifespan that is genetically predetermined? According to experts, those of us with healthy genes and good lifestyle habits will live until the age of eighty-five, so long as unexpected illness and disease does not interfere with normal health. Some of us will live well beyond that. Based on census figures there's already a significant rise in the number of centenarians. In fact, the U.S. Census Bureau projects that by the middle of this century, there will be eleven times as many people one hundred years or older than there are now.

Although human lifespan is programmed, we all have the capacity to maximize that lifespan through activities that keep the mind-body connection strong and healthy. We've come a long way since the days of the Roman Empire when people lived an average of twenty-five years. The typical life expectancy in developed countries is now eighty or more years, and there's no reason, according to some experts, that humans cannot live to an age of one hundred twenty.

PSYCHOLOGICAL STRESS
OF AGING

Unlike biological aging, which is the result of basic genetic and physical mechanisms, psychological aging depends on a lifetime of experiences, which condition us to perceive events and then respond to them in certain ways. And while biological aging involves the death of cells and the deterioration of bodily functions, psychological aging involves the death of positive attitudes and behaviors. This change in how we view life is what causes us to experience severe stress reactions and makes us susceptible to serious and debilitating mental health problems as we age.

When a survey was taken by the National Council on Aging, there was a great discrepancy between what younger people thought about the elderly and what the elderly thought about themselves. According to the survey, older people who are nearing retirement report having positive self-images, being able to adapt well to change and being a valuable part of society. Several years after retirement, however, there's a tendency for those positive self-images to decline. For those who have not prepared themselves for the sudden loss of activity, the self-image is much worse.

The difference between how older people think of themselves and how younger members of society think of them leads to "self-fulfilling prophecies" in which adverse beliefs about aging cause lowered expectations, negative attitudes and poor health. This causes older individuals to doubt their own worth and to perceive aging through the eyes of younger people. When that happens, they take on a distorted view of themselves and become more despondent and prone to stress effects. The fear, depression and anxiety of growing old in this kind of environment invariably leads to tremendous emotional strain which intensifies the stress response.

As we age, our mental health really depends on how successfully we adapt to life events as well as on our own personality type. According to some age researchers, personality is the pivotal factor in predicting which individuals will age successfully (i.e. with good physical and mental health) and which will be more susceptible to age-related health disorders. That's because personality is the key element in our ability to come to terms with life experiences and situations.

The individual most likely to age successfully is one who can reach a high level of life satisfaction through his or her ability to interact with others and to become involved in outside activities. In other words, the person who can find and utilize support systems and other effective avenues of coping has a better chance of aging well. Regardless of how old we are, most of us can't cope as well by ourselves as we can when we surround ourselves with others. The lesson we've learned from age-related studies is that support networks and outside activities are a critical part of stress management in the elderly and can actually slow down the aging process.

Outside activities are an excellent way to replace the loss of a friend, a loved one or a job. Very often, the difference between successful and unsuccessful aging is our willingness to accept loss and a desire to adapt to changes and challenges. In order to help the adaptation process, older individuals need to maintain physical movement, social interaction, emotionally and intellectually stimulating activities and self-care capabilities. Without these, there's social isolation, physical disability, frustration and apathy. These, in turn, can lead to depression and, in the worse case, suicide.

MIND, BODY AND STRESS
HORMONES DURING AGING

The stress hormones discussed in earlier chapters are so called because they're released during stress and help our bodies' defense against negative stress reactions. But as we age, these stress hormones begin to act on our bodies in different ways and they make the response to stress more acute and much more damaging. When released, they interact with normal aging processes and gradually create a climate that can speed up cell death, disease formation and the loss of general bodily functions. In essence, while stress hormones are vital for survival, they also contribute to the acceleration of aging.

Another important aspect of aging is the possibility that "brain aging" may act as a pacemaker or trigger for other forms of aging, because of changes in the way these hormones regulate the central nervous system. Studies done at the Bowman Gray School of Medicine, for example, suggest that stress hormones may be responsible for some of the changes that take place within the brain during aging. Researchers found that blood levels of stress hormones correlate significantly with the degree of age-related brain changes and that there is an acceleration of structural changes in the brains of young animals very much like changes experienced during aging. More recent studies show that when animals have their source of stress hormones, i.e. adrenal glands, surgically removed, they show fewer signs of brain aging than do other animals of the same age.

In a related study, researchers at the Jewish Hospital in Cincinnati found that the tempo of modern living, as well as physical stress, can alter internal body chemistry and lead to premature blood vessel disease and aging. The results of the study showed that the overactivity of glands that regulate hormone responses to stress may lead to illnesses and diseases normally found in aged individuals. So despite the dramatic increase in life expectancy, the intensified demands of modern living, together with stress hormones associated with them, may actually be contributing to accelerated aging.

But exactly what is it about stress hormones and stress reactions that cause the brain to change and make us age faster than we should? The answer may lie in the hippocampus—the same area of the brain discussed in earlier chapters as being a center for learning and memory. It turns out that another important function of the hippocampus is the regulation of glucocorticoids, the stress hormones most responsible for negative health effects when produced in excess. Here is the chain of events that could very well play the key role in immune system breakdown and premature aging:

- Chronic stress triggers CRF from the hypothalamus, which then stimulates release of ACTH

- ACTH stimulates the adrenal cortex to secrete glucocorticoids, particularly cortisol

- Glucocorticoids not only make the body more prone to diabetes, osteoporosis, and a breakdown in immune function, they also damage the hippocampus

- Damage to the hippocampus disrupts the normal feedback system which regulates glucocorticoids

- Excess glucocorticoid secretion further damages the hippocampus and makes one even more susceptible to disease and immune breakdown

- Disease and immune breakdown lead to physical and emotional stress reactions which cause release of glucocorticoids and even more damage to the hippocampus

Besides glucose and excess cortisol, there is one other hormone that wreaks havoc on aging systems and actually accelerates the aging process. That's insulin. Elevated insulin levels—caused by overeating, especially eating too many carbohydrates—stimulates the body to release more cortisol. And by now we all know the kind of damage cortisol can do to cells and to immune function in general.

Excess insulin drives blood sugar out of the circulatory system and into our cells. Unfortunately, this prevents glucose from getting to our brain, which relies almost solely on sugar to nourish it. In response, the body produces large amounts of cortisol in an effort to quickly balance glucose levels. The end result is more cortisol in our system, depressed immune function and damage to cells and organ systems.

The best way to prevent this from happening is to (1) limit calorie intake, specifically empty carbohydrate-type foods that trigger release of insulin and have little or no nutritional value, (2) increase exercise, which reduces insulin levels and increases the number of insulin receptors, thus making cells more efficient at responding to insulin, and (3) practice relaxation techniques which reduce cortisol levels in general. According to age researchers, we can significantly slow down the aging process and keep our immune system healthy if we just follow those three rules. By focusing on cortisol and insulin in particular, experts say, we'll grow old in the best possible way and improve every aspect of our health and well-being.

DIET, NUTRITION AND AGING

Some of the physical and psychological changes we experience as we grow older are certainly influenced by the habits and conditionings of a lifetime. The foods we eat, the amount of exercise we get and the kinds of lifestyles we lead all influence how well the mind-body connection works during our golden years. Based on mounds of evidence over the last decade, we now know that, together with genes and lifestyle, nutrition is a key factor in the aging process.

Why do people change their eating habits and get fewer nutrients as they age? One reason is that during aging there's a decrease in the number of taste buds and olfactory (smell) receptors, so food just doesn't taste the same as it once did. As a result, the elderly tend to eat less, season their food more with salt or sugar, and consume less healthy foods. But there's another reason. Stress.

Nutrition and stress are linked during aging, because people naturally change their eating habits as they become stressed more often. A cycle begins in which age-related stress leads to illness and emotional problems, which cause poor eating habits, which in turn lead to more illness and even greater stress.

As we get older, the rate at which our bodies absorb nutrients and use energy decreases. This is made even worse by stressful situations such as loneliness, depression, poor teeth, illness, income limitations and increased medicine use. Weak gums and teeth make chewing more difficult, which results in diets limited to foods that are easy to chew, but which may be lacking in essential nutrients. These kinds of poor eating habits can alter blood levels of stress hormones, affect the aging process and lead to age-related illness and disease.

In order to keep the mind and the body as healthy as possible during the aging process, we need to be more concerned about nutrition. Certain foods improve memory and help nerve cells grow, thereby keeping us mentally sharp. An added bonus to keeping the brain healthy is that the brain, in turn, will keep the body healthy. In a later section, I'll discuss specific foods, supplements and brain exercises that enhance mental fitness.

AGING AND MENTAL FITNESS

Medical textbooks prior to 1970 reported that when brain cells die they are lost forever. We now know that, like other cells in the body, nerve cells in the brain regenerate, especially when we think or use our mind to solve problems. So, simply by thinking, we stimulate the growth of new brain cells and neural networks.

At the present time, there's no evidence at all that aging produces a change in intelligence, learning capacity, memory or information processing. In fact, while some special skills aren't performed as successfully after the age of forty, intellectual functions that rely on the application of learned material remain intact well into our seventies.

This was clearly demonstrated in a twenty-one-year study conducted at the University of Southern California's gerontology research institute, which found that subjects ranging from ages twenty-two to eighty-one all maintained their level of intellectual competence—or actually improved—as they grew older. In fact, even between the ages of seventy-four and eighty-one, about 10 percent of the subjects tested performed better intellectually over the twenty-one-year period than they had at younger ages.

In another study done at the University of Rochester, researchers found that aged brains had longer and more extensive nerve fibers within the cortex than did brains of younger individuals. Since nerve fibers in the cortex provide information to the area of the brain responsible for learning and memory, it seems that the capacity for processing information continues despite age. The point at which brain nerve degeneration begins to overtake nerve growth has not been determined yet, since the oldest brain studied was ninety-two years old and still had an extensive network of nerve fibers.

The final piece of evidence, however, has now been presented by researchers at Princeton University's brain research team. Until recently, most neurobiologists held the belief that the brain's learning and memory centers only grew new neurons early in life, then stopped, only to begin reversing the process. What was lost, so to speak, was lost forever. The Princeton team, for the first time, actually traced the path followed by neurons created in the part of the mature brain responsible for reasoning, intelligence and thinking. What they discovered and published in the journal *Science* was a naturally regenerative mechanism that repopulates neurons and incorporates them into the existing thinking center.

These and other aging studies have proven once and for all that intelligence doesn't peak at an early age and then declines as one grows older. On the contrary, these studies show that neural connections can regenerate and may actually grow faster when the brain is used. The good news is that the capacity to learn is a lifelong process and a good reason for older people to remain active and productive throughout their lives.

That said, there is also evidence that if the brain is abused or not used, it can lose a significant number of nerve cells per day. In order to slow brain aging, older people should maintain high levels of physical and mental activity. Some of the greatest writers, painters, musicians, scientists, and scholars in history have done their best work well past their sixties. We need to follow that example and never allow age to get in the way of our ambitions, dreams or goals. Here are some suggestions on how we can improve brain function, creativity and memory well into old age:

- **Exercise the brain.** The adage "if you don't use it, you'll lose it" is as true for the brain as it is for the muscles in your body. Anything that stimulates brain cells and makes you think is good. Solving puzzles or cryptograms, working out problems, reading, writing, taking classes, learning new hobbies or musical instruments and even playing games like scrabble or chess will exercise the mind and slow down memory loss.

- **Exercise the body.** Recent studies at Harvard, Yale, Duke and Mt. Sinai School of Medicine showed that one of the key factors in maintaining good brain function is physical exercise. The reason is simple. Exercise increases heart rate, which brings more oxygen to the brain. Since oxygen is vital in cell and tissue repair, energy production and overall mental and physical health, a steady flow of oxygen—even through moderate exercise such as walking 20 minutes a day—will do wonders for mental fitness.

- **Consume brain foods.** Besides eating a well-balanced diet that includes five servings of fruit and vegetables a day and all the necessary vitamins and minerals, older people should also eat more foods that specifically boost their brain power, especially foods containing DHA (Docosahexaenoic acid). DHA helps maintain cell membranes, which are important in nerve and brain function. According to researchers, individuals with high brain DHA levels tend to have better memories and mental capacity. Foods with the highest levels of DHA are ocean fish such as salmon, halibut, herring, mackerel, bluefin tuna, sardines, anchovies, and striped bass. If you don't like fish, try a fish oil supplement containing DHA. Also proven to stave off age-related memory loss is olive oil and colorful produce such as carrots, sweet potatoes and broccoli.

- **Try some herbal memory boosters.** For centuries, herbs have been used to sharpen mental skills, enhance focus and improve memory. Recent studies have had mixed results, but there are certain herbal products that seem to hold promise when it comes to boosting memory, either directly or as a result of improved circulation, which brings oxygen to the brain. According to some experts, the ones that seem to work best are: basil, flaxseed oil, ginkgo biloba, ginseng and rosemary.

- **Take more Vitamin E.** Several research studies have shown that vitamin E helps keep the mind sharp during aging. An added benefit is that it also reduces the risk of certain types of cancer and helps fight the damaging effects of diabetes. In one study of 3,000 people age sixty-five and older at St. Luke's Medical Center in Chicago, researchers found that those who'd taken 300IU of vitamin E a day had significantly decreased memory loss and improved mental function in general compared to those not taking vitamin E supplements. Since most average diets include very low vitamin E levels, older people should either take supplements or eat more high vitamin E foods such as nuts, peanut butter and sunflower seeds.

- **Watch those medications.** Drug interactions can affect the senses of older people so much that symptoms are sometimes mistaken for dementia. If you notice changes in memory or concentration a few weeks after starting a new medication, talk to your doctor at once about changing the prescription or altering the dosage.

- **Monitor your health.** As we get older, our glands and organs don't function as well as they once did and our bodies aren't as efficient at producing hormones, red blood cells and hemoglobin. Our memory problems or lack of concentration may be nothing more than anemia, low hemoglobin levels, an under active thyroid or a host of other minor health disorders that are easily measured and easily treated. In many cases, a simple iron pill or a prescription medication will completely reverse a memory disorder.

- **Get lost for a while.** The stress of life is a brain drain. It saps our energy levels and depresses brain function. So take a trip, go on vacation or simply get lost by yourself in a quiet room to meditate, do yoga or just chill for fifteen minutes a day.

The evidence that stress and glitches in the mind-body connection can indeed accelerate the aging process is beginning to mount. As more and more long-term studies are done, it's becoming clear that stress reactions, especially stress hormone reactions, contribute to the deterioration of body tissues, breakdown of immune function and homeostatic mechanisms, susceptibility to disease and acceleration of age-related structural changes in the brain. It's also clear that stress-induced activities and habits such as poor eating, smoking, drinking, improper drug use, etc. contribute significantly to the overall aging process.

As we get older, we need to be more aware of stress responses and not treat them simply as normal aging symptoms. By using coping strategies, adopting good health habits, eating properly, belonging to social groups and practicing relaxation exercises, we can actually slow down the aging process and live out our lives in the healthiest way possible. The idea, after all, is not only to live as long as we can, but to live out our lives in the healthiest way possible.

COPING WITH DEATH
AND DYING

From the minute we're born we begin to die. Even though as youngsters we grow and develop rapidly, we proceed nonetheless on a slow and irrevocable journey toward the end of our lives. As we get older, death becomes more real and more certain. The deaths of friends, relatives, and acquaintances continually reminds us of our own mortality and makes us realize that we too must someday face the inevitable.

Encounters with death or dying are very stressful experiences not only for the person who is dying, but also for those of us who must cope with the grief of actually witnessing someone we love go through the dying process.

Each person is different. Those of us who don't cope well with other crises probably will have trouble dealing with our own death, as well as the death of someone close to us.

If we're grieving for someone we love, a decrease in immunity can cause us to become much more susceptible to disease. It is not uncommon for individuals to become seriously ill following the death of a spouse. There are several techniques for establishing :60 second managements both for coping with your own grief and the grief of others.

:60 SECOND MANAGEMENTS FOR COPING WITH YOUR OWN GRIEF

1. *Express your emotions.* Crying, remembering and talking are all part of a healthy grieving process and shouldn't be suppressed for the sake of "appearing strong." Normal grieving may take as long as a year or longer, but some individuals may go through short periods of grief for the rest of their lives. They describe their pain and loss as something that will be a part of their memories always, even though they resume otherwise normal and meaningful lives. Psychotherapists have found that by expressing your feelings early and allowing your normal grieving process to happen quickly and naturally, you'll recover more rapidly and, more importantly, you'll resume a healthy and emotionally satisfying life.

2. *Seek out social support.* Grief often is intensified when we have to experience it alone. This doesn't mean you have to join every support group you can find. But you need to allow others to help you and give comfort to you even if it's just in the form of a brief visit. It's normal to want time alone with your grief, to recall memories and to think about what has happened in your life. But the worst thing to do, especially during the early stages of grief, is to become isolated and withdrawn from those who are willing to give you needed support. It has been found, for example, that women seem to cope better following a death, because they tend to seek out support more often than men.

3. *Seek professional help.* Most of us who grieve will never need professional counseling. There is, however, a condition called "pathologic grief" in which bereavement becomes permanently stuck in the middle of the grieving process. We need to watch for symptoms like excessive grief after a year of our loss, avoidance of anything associated with the death, severe anxiety and

depression. If your grief is not subsiding normally and is, in fact, causing you to exhibit severe emotional symptoms, you need to get professional help in order to get through the grieving process and to keep you from developing even worse emotional problems.

:60 SECOND
MANAGEMENTS FOR
HELPING OTHERS TO
COPE WITH GRIEF

1. *Be present.* Even though you may feel helpless in these situations, just your being there will be enough to give comfort. Someone who is grieving is more prone to depression, suicide and emotional breakdowns and shouldn't be left alone for long periods of time. And even though grieving individuals want to spend time alone with their thoughts and emotions, they really do need support and love during the grieving process. An arm around a shoulder or a hug can mean all the difference in the world during an especially lonely moment.

2. *Be a good listener.* Part of a healthy grieving process is talking through feelings about death and dying. Rather than discourage a grieving individual's attempts to discuss death, listen and encourage an open and frank discussion of what has occurred. Talking actually can help speed up the grieving process and make recovery much less painful. When listening to a grieving person, never interrupt and say things like, "It was really for the best," "There was nothing anybody could have done," or "Now you can get on with your life." Try to be sensitive to the person's feelings, allowing him or her to verbalize grief without interrupting with statements that you think will lessen the impact of death.

3. *Be a source of activity.* Often times, a grieving individual needs to get away and do things that will take his or her mind off the tragedy. Invite your friend for dinner, for a game of cards, to a movie, for a walk, to a concert, to a ballgame, etc. In some cases, it takes just a small push by someone who cares to get a grieving individual back on track and on the way to a speedy recovery.

4. *Be a continued source of support.* It's great to be a comfort to

grieving friends when a death occurs. It's just as important to be there for them on a long-term basis. For many grieving individuals, the worst time following a death is the first anniversary or the first major holiday spent alone. To be a true source of support, you need to remember your friends on these critical occasions and invite them to dinner or to spend the day with you. If your friends want to talk about their grief, let them share their feelings and express themselves again. Your presence will reaffirm to them that they're not alone and can depend on friends for continued support.

:60 SECOND STRESS MANAGEMENTS FOR THE ELDERLY

Stress management for the elderly must include coping strategies that deal specifically with loneliness, physical disability, rejection and feelings of worthlessness. Emotional stresses such as these are so powerful that older people often find it impossible to live or cope in a society that looks at them in any kind of negative way. Unless something is done, the stress of aging can become a destructive mental and physical process.

There's no question that social conditions affect physical ability and independence and contribute enormously to the health of older people. The elderly, living alone in areas where there's no social organization for them, increase their chances of succumbing to illness and disease. On the other hand, older people belonging to religious groups or close ethnic groups are buffered against stress-related disease, because they exist within a well-integrated community. In essence, they have many social and community ties.

For some time, social isolation has been suspected of increasing the aging process. In one study, for example, it was found that people lacking social ties had three times the mortality rate over a ten-year period than people having close social ties. Being involved in social and community affairs, giving and seeking advice and other forms of assistance had an important effect on how older people perceived their own health status. Furthermore, having close friends and confidants had a strong tendency to relieve stress and influence both physical and mental health. In another study, it was shown that the stresses of retirement, death of a spouse and decreased activity were lessened as a result of having supportive exchanges with an intimate friend.

Social support networks, then, serve to bring us back from isolation into a social community that will respond to our needs and offer us an outlet for sharing, communicating and interacting. Some of the best social support networks are religious organizations, retirement associations and clubs, volunteer and charity organizations and community action groups. These kinds of support groups can enrich our lives by making us feel useful and needed and by giving us a sense of dignity. Aging, after all, doesn't necessarily mean an end to our challenges but the beginning of a new phase of our lives in which we fulfill those challenges in a different but equally enthusiastic and satisfying way.

There are several coping strategies which will lead to :60 second stress managements that can help older people deal with the stress in their lives and slow down the aging process.

1. *Participate in "enrichment programs."* These activities are a way to increase self-esteem and achieve something worthwhile.

2. *Participate in sporting activities and exercises.* Exercise helps us boost our energy reserves and triggers the release of endorphins, which help us cope with both physical and mental stress.

3. *Obtain proper health care.* Minor health problems can lead to major health disorders. Never assume any kind of physical or mental illness is a normal byproduct of age.

4. *Get a pet.* Pets satisfy needs such as caring for others and a desire to be loved and needed. Animals fulfill the human craving for emotional relationships and promote interactions and involvement.

5. *Improve eating habits.* Eating right can have an anti-aging effect on the body. You'll experience fewer stress reactions, and live a lot better.

6. *Eliminate destructive habits.* Smoking and alcohol consumption can be deadly for older people, since they can adversely affect the reaction of prescribed drug medications. Adverse drug reactions lead to negative stress reactions which can encourage even more smoking and drinking.

7. *Exercise the brain.* Some of the best writers, poets, painters,

musicians, scientists and scholars are well past their sixties. We should never allow age to get in the way of our ambitions.

The evidence that stress can indeed accelerate the aging process is only now beginning to accumulate. As more and more long-term studies are done, it's becoming clear that stress reactions, especially stress hormone reactions, contribute to the deterioration of body tissues, breakdown of immune function, susceptibility to illness and disease and acceleration of age-related structural changes in the brain. It's also clear that stress-induced activities and habits such as poor eating, smoking, drinking, improper drug use, etc. also have a tremendous negative influence on the overall aging process.

As we get older we need to be more aware of stress responses and be wary not to treat them as just "normal aging symptoms." By using coping strategies, maintaining good health habits, eating properly, belonging to social support groups and practicing relaxation exercises, we can actually slow down the aging process and live out our lives in the healthiest way possible.

· PART II ·

RELAXATION TECHNIQUES AND EXERCISES

Introduction

We have learned what happens to us during periods stress and how stress reactions can bring about many kinds of illnesses and disease. We have discovered how our own habits shape our behavior patterns and how we can establish :60 second management reactions.

There are various relaxation exercises that are the mainstay of any stress management strategy. No amount of attitude or behavior modification can totally replace relaxation as an effective tool for relieving stress. We know that what we do within the first few minutes of a stress reaction sets into motion the mechanisms of physical response. It is during these few seconds that we have the ability to change that response from a negative and destructive "stress response" to a positive and beneficial "relaxation response." Encouragingly, the relaxation response is just as natural as the stress response.

Our goal has been to develop and evoke that relaxation response so that it becomes a :60 second management that is instantly and automatically available in a time of need.

The principal relaxation exercises are progressive muscle relaxation (PMR), tension relaxation, meditation and imaging. Once practiced and learned, relaxation exercises can bring our body back to a state of relaxation within sixty seconds, after which we can continue to relax for as long as we choose. Learning to eliminate negative stress reactions is the key element behind :60 second stress management.

· Chapter 9 ·

Progressive Muscle Relaxation
(PMR)

The principal behind relaxation training is that tension is incompatible with relaxation. Relaxation exercises produce a feeling of well-being and rest by creating a relaxed state that actually inhibits anxiety and negative stress reactions. In other words, we either do one or the other. Whenever we relax our mind and our body, we automatically exclude the stress that produces muscular tension.

The degree to which our muscles are relaxed can be controlled by practicing a special technique called progressive muscle relaxation or PMR. In PMR, the objective is to induce deep muscular relaxation by gradually releasing tension from various parts of the body, one part at a time.

There are three basic positions which facilitate any kind of relaxation exercise, including PMR. These are the lying position (figure 9a), the sitting position (figure 9b) and the semi-reclining position (figure 9c). The sitting position is useful whenever we're at work or any other place where lying down isn't possible. Most beginners find that lying down is the most effective position because it often already evokes the relaxation response. After learning a relaxation technique, any position can be equally effective and satisfying.

Regardless of which position is used, comfort is absolutely critical. Pillows should be placed under the head, knees and arms as shown in figure 9a, or under the face, pelvis and feet if we're lying down. In the semi-reclining position, the chair should be soft and comfortable and have cushioned arms. If necessary, the forearms may be supported by placing pillows on the chair arms. The feet also need to be supported, either by a footrest or a pillow. The head must be in a comfortable position and supported by a chair, cushion or pillow. Unless the body is totally comfortable, relaxation will be possible, but won't be as effec-

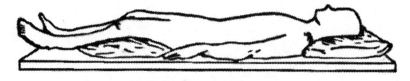

Figure 9a: Lying Down

Figure 9b: Sitting

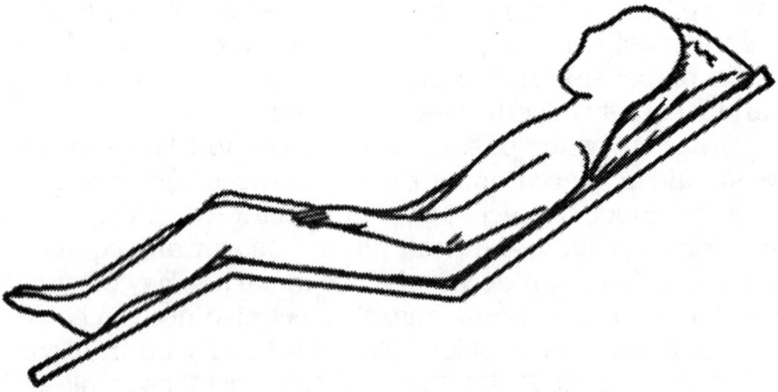

Figure 9c: Semi-reclining

tive. Therefore, body position and comfort are the principle starting points to begin any relaxation exercise.

Some people have found that music is also a big factor in helping them relax, because they can concentrate on the music and forget about other distractions. When listening to music, however, make sure that it's not too loud and never too harsh. Good music for relaxation is any type of soft music that's soothing and melodic.

After assuming a comfortable position, either sitting in a chair or lying down, take your shoes off, close your eyes and begin by concentrating on your muscle groups one at a time, starting with your toes first. Here's a sample of the kind of self-instruction you can use to produce a relaxed state. After using these instructions several times, you'll know them by heart and be able to use them automatically whenever you feel tense. You may even want to shorten your self-instructions after becoming adept at bringing on relaxation. As you begin to condition yourself to relax, you'll notice that relaxation will come more quickly and with much less effort each time. With enough practice, you'll be able to relax your entire body within a minute.

PMR Self-Instructions

I'm falling into a nice, relaxed state; I'm breathing deeply, slowly and smoothly...deeply, slowly and smoothly. As I breathe, I'm becoming more and more relaxed...relaxed...relaxed. The toes on my feet are becoming numb; I feel a tingling sensation as the muscles in my toes become more relaxed and tension free...relaxed and tension free. They're getting more and more numb and heavy as I breathe. Each breath I take makes my toes become heavier and more numb...heavier and more numb. Now my toes are very heavy...very heavy...very heavy. The heavy, numb sensation is making my toes feel totally relaxed...relaxed...relaxed...more relaxed with each breath I take.

The numbness is beginning to creep up from my toes to my feet. My feet are beginning to tingle as they get heavy and numb...heavy and numb. There's a slight burning sensation in my feet as if they were submerged in warm, refreshing water. As I breathe, I can feel my feet becoming more numb and more relaxed. The muscles in both feet are becoming loose and soft...loose and soft; they feel very warm, heavy and relaxed...relaxed...relaxed...more relaxed with each breath I take. My feet are so warm and soft...warm and soft...relaxed...relaxed...relaxed... more relaxed with each breath I take.

I feel the warmth and numbness going to my calves as I breathe and relax...breathe and relax. My calves are beginning to get very heavy and numb...heavy and numb. They're getting soft and warm as tension leaves and my muscles relax...relax...relax. With each breath I take, my calves are getting heavier and heavier...heavier and heavier, relaxed and numb, tension free and relaxed...relaxed...relaxed...more relaxed with each breath I take. The warmth is soothing and refreshing...soothing and refreshing, relaxed...relaxed...relaxed...more relaxed with each breath I take.

The numbness is going from my calves to my thighs. My thighs are now beginning to get warm and soft...warm and soft...loose and relaxed...loose and relaxed. My thighs are getting numb and heavy...numb and heavy; there's a tingling sensation as they become more numb and heavy...soft and relaxed...soft and relaxed. With each breath I take, my thighs are getting heavier...heavier...heavier. I feel the warmth and numbness creeping up my thighs and releasing tension. With each breath I take, my thighs feel more and more relaxed... relaxed...relaxed...more relaxed with each breath I take.

My fingers are beginning to tingle and get numb as the warmth creeps into them. They're becoming soft and loose...soft and loose, warm and numb...numb...numb. I sense a numbness going from the tips of my fingers into my knuckles as I breathe slowly and relax...relax...relax. The warmth and numbness is going into my wrists and my wrists are getting warmer and warmer, softer and softer. My hands are heavy and relaxed...heavy and relaxed. With each breath I take my hands are heavy and relaxed...relaxed...relaxed...more relaxed with each breath I take.

My arms are now beginning to get numb. The warmth is going from my hands into my arms and I feel heaviness and warmth...heaviness and warmth. As I breathe, my arms are getting heavier and heavier, numb and relaxed...numb and relaxed. A tingling and numbing sensation is going up my arms and releasing tension; my muscles are beginning to relax...relax...relax. My arms are very heavy now and relaxed...relaxed...relaxed...more relaxed with each breath I take.

The numbness in my arms is going into my shoulders. My shoulders are getting heavy and numb...heavy and numb. I can feel the warmth and heaviness loosening the muscles in my shoulders and they're getting more relaxed...relaxed...relaxed...more relaxed with each breath I take. As I breathe, tension is leaving my shoulders. They now feel very warm and numb...warm and numb, heavy and relaxed...relaxed...more relaxed with each breath I take.

Warmth is spreading from my shoulders into my chest. My chest feels warmer and warmer...looser and looser. With each breath I take, my chest is becoming heavy and numb...heavy and numb, soft and relaxed... relaxed... relaxed. I can feel the muscles in my chest tingle and become numb and heavy...numb and heavy. As I breathe, tension is leaving and my chest is relaxed...relaxed...relaxed...more relaxed with each breath I take. My chest feels very heavy and numb now. With each breath I take, my chest is relaxed...relaxed...relaxed... relaxed.

The numbness and warmth are traveling from my chest to my neck. My neck is becoming warm and numb...warm and numb. I can feel the tingling, numbing feeling in my neck as I breathe and relax...relax...relax...relax. My neck is getting heavier and heavier... warmer and warmer...more relaxed with each breath I take. The tension is leaving the muscles in my neck and my neck is relaxed...relaxed...relaxed...more relaxed with each breath I take.

My face is getting softer and softer...softer and softer. The warmth is spreading from my neck into my face and it's getting warmer... warmer...warmer. As I breathe, my face is becoming heavier and heavier...relaxed and tension free. I feel all the tension leaving my facial muscles and they're becoming relaxed...relaxed...relaxed...more relaxed with each breath I take.

My body feels warm and relaxed...relaxed...relaxed; heavy and numb...heavy and numb. My body is so heavy and relaxed that it's sinking into the chair. Tension is melting away; my body muscles are soft and relaxed...soft and relaxed, heavy and limp...heavy and limp. As I breathe, I feel a soothing warmth and I'm relaxed...relaxed...relaxed. Tension is flowing away; with each breath I take, I can relax...relax... relax...relax...relax...relax.

This is only a sample of the kind of self-instruction you can use to relax yourself. You may use anything that comes to your mind, providing it elicits a pattern of gradual relaxation throughout your body. You also can continue and prolong the instructions so that you set your own pace and bring about relaxation in your own way. When using PMR, however, there are several things you should remember in order to enhance the technique. These are:

1. *Always make comfort the starting point of relaxation.* Remove your shoes and tight-fitting clothing, loosen your belt and take off any jewelry that might distract you when you come to that particular body part. Don't try to practice relaxation in a room that's too cold or too hot. Remember, anything that can distract you probably will.

2. *Speak to yourself in a slow, rhythmic and monotonous manner.* This helps get you into a comfortable and steady pace, which facilitates relaxation.

3. *Breathe slowly and rhythmically.* To make sure you're breathing properly, try this exercise. Place your right hand on your upper abdomen just above your navel and your left hand in the middle of your upper chest, just above your nipples. When you breathe, the right hand should rise as you inhale and fall as you exhale;

the left hand shouldn't move at all. After a few practice sessions, you should be able to breathe this way while having your hands at your sides in a relaxed state.

Don't exhale all your breath at the beginning of each breath cycle. The last thing you want to do is gasp for air. Make sure that each breath is long and even, smooth and gentle. This rhythmic smoothness allows our autonomic nervous system to take over and keep us relaxed and tension free. When giving repeated self-instructions such as "relax...relax...relax," say each word slowly at the same speed and smoothness as your exhaling breath.

4. Use "soft" words like relax, soothing, smooth, heavy, limp, numb, etcetera. Avoid words that are harsh and make you feel tense or lose concentration.

5. Don't go on to the next body part until the part you're working on is completely relaxed.

6. When your body is completely relaxed, allow yourself to remain that way for several minutes before getting up to stretch.

THE IMPORTANCE OF BREATHING

For centuries, practitioners of meditation, such as Buddhist monks, yogis and Indian gurus have relied on proper breathing techniques to maximize the effects of meditation. Doctors have also helped their patients supplement more traditional treatments for aches and pains through the use of breathing and meditation. The manner in which one breathes during relaxation is very important, because of the close relationship between the respiratory and central nervous systems.

It's well known that breathing rates and breathing patterns have a profound effect on brain waves that, in turn, influence both our emotional and physical processes. Improper or intermittent breathing, for example, can disrupt biochemical reactions, alter emotional states and create anxiety. Conversely, proper breathing can be used to relieve chronic pain and soothe other discomforts that could interfere with relaxation. For this reason, an integral part of any meditative exercise is properly controlled breathing, which can actually speed up the healing process for those in physical therapy or who are convalescing.

Done properly, the physical act of breathing is the thread that links the mind to the body and brings us back to a state of equilibrium. From the moment we're born to the day we take our last breath, we experience life through breathing. We gasp, yawn, scream, yell, hold our breath with excitement or anticipation, vent our feelings and sigh with emotion. We whisper in one another's ears and open our lips to form billions of words in a lifetime. We think more clearly and boost our energy levels when we allow our brain to take in more oxygen. If there's a single human act we do that gives us life and keeps us healthy, it is breathing.

Besides the positive effects on meditation and self-healing, the energy derived from proper breathing can minimize the effects of aging and has been shown to slow the wear and tear on the body caused by age. Whenever blood flow is enhanced or extra oxygen is supplied to soft tissues throughout the body, there's an increase in the speed of cell regeneration and a reversal of damage created by poor circulation and low oxygen levels. In other words, proper breathing by itself can make us feel better and younger.

The breathing exercises in this chapter are important to meditation and stress relief because they help bring balance between the central nervous and respiratory systems. In order to achieve deep relaxation, we need to ensure that these two systems are in synch, with the central nervous system subconsciously controlling the flow and rhythm of our breathing patterns. Combined with meditation, correct breathing is one of the most effective tools in helping us relax and replenish our lost energy. The following are simple breathing exercises.

Diaphragm Breathing

While sitting in a meditative position, place your right hand on your diaphragm just above your waist and your left hand on your upper chest. As you breath deeply and slowly, your right hand should be pushed out and in with each inhalation and exhalation while your left hand remains steady. If you're breathing properly, air will travel into your body without disrupting the muscles in your chest cavity. The advantage here is that this type of breathing, which is smoother and more rhythmic than chest breathing, facilitates concentration and induces relaxation because it's more natural and requires less work.

When practicing diaphragm breathing, make certain that your breaths are smooth and even, without pauses, jerks or altered tempo and with your tongue pushed slightly forward so that it touches the teeth. The smoother your breathing, the more effectively the rest of your body will respond and relax. With a little effort and practice, you'll be able to change your "unnatural" habit of chest breathing to a more "natural" habit of diaphragm breathing.

Timed Breathing

There are two ways to practice timed breathing, both of which improve breath control and enhance relaxation. Whether you use one or both methods, you should make an effort to practice regularly in order to condition yourself to inhale and exhale the right way automatically.

Uneven Breathing

In contrast to regular, even breathing, which involves inhalation and exhalation of the same length, uneven breathing requires that you exhale for longer periods of time than you inhale. You do this by slowing down the rate of exhalation until it's approximately two to three times as long as the rate of inhalation. For example, without changing the smoothness or rhythm of your breathing pattern, inhale for two seconds and exhale for four, or inhale for two and exhale for six. However you do it, make breathing effortless, minimizing even the pauses between inhalation and exhalation.

Deep Breathing

This exercise will help increase your breath and body control, which in turn will lead to deeper relaxation and tension relief. Take a deep breath (four to six seconds), using your diaphragm, and hold it for a full ten seconds. Then, after taking a few regular breaths, take a deep breath and, while holding it, pull your diaphragm back into your spine as far as you can for a full ten seconds. Remember to breathe smoothly and effortlessly each time you exhale or inhale.

One final point about deep breathing as a meditative tool: to achieve a proper breathing pattern, it's important that there be no tension in the neck or shoulder muscles. Otherwise, the tension will run down to the abdomen and interfere with inhalation and exhalation. So before starting a breathing or meditative exercise, it's a good idea to roll your head gently back and forth, actually feeling the tension melting away. Dangle your head for a moment toward the floor. Then make large circles as you count slowly and breathe deeply. Once you feel that your neck muscles are relaxed, dangle your arms and make slow round circles with your shoulders. Don't begin meditating until you feel that the tension is gone.

Progressive muscle relaxation has been very effective in relieving a variety of stress-related illnesses such as hypertension, migraine headaches and ulcers. But even if we don't suffer from these kinds of illnesses, it may be necessary to use this technique several times a day if we're in severe stress situations. After a short while, relaxation will become much easier and almost spontaneous. We'll have conditioned ourselves to bring on the relaxation response just as we would any other natural, physiologic reaction. Once we learn how our muscles should feel when they're relaxed, it becomes nothing more than a matter of habit and conditioning to bring them into that relaxed state whenever we want to. When we can do that, taking part in challenging and exciting activities will become much more enjoyable, because we'll never have to fear the threat of muscle tension again.

Chapter 10

Tension / Relaxation

The principle behind tension/relaxation is to familiarize our bodies and minds with what tension should feel like as compared with relaxation. This simple and easily learned procedure consists of conscious muscular tension followed immediately by relaxation.

The positions for the tension/relaxation technique are the same as those used for Progressive Muscle Relaxation and it remains important to be as comfortable as possible and not have any distractions or disturbances during the exercises. After practicing this technique daily for several weeks, the conditioning process will take over and our responses will become easier and more automatic. Habits form that enable our muscles to relax at will, regardless of the positions we assume. The key element in shaping this conditioned response is our brain's innate ability to recognize degrees of physical tension and then to respond to that tension by relaxing the muscles almost involuntarily.

When first starting tension/relaxation exercises, different muscle groups are tensed individually during separate exercise sessions. These are: hands, arms, legs, chest, back, shoulders, neck and forehead. Only after the individual muscle groups are mastered should you put the technique together and use it to relax all the muscle groups in one session. By practicing the technique for each separate body region, the conditioning process is much more effective and total body relaxation will become much easier. Later, some of the muscle groups, such as hands and arms and shoulders and neck, can be combined so that relaxation is achieved by concentrating on only a few muscle groups.

Eventually, the "tension" part of tension/relaxation can be eliminated altogether, because relaxation will become a classically conditioned response. You'll be able to relax your entire body at once or only the specific parts of your body that are especially tense.

A word of caution, however: always be aware of your ability to recognize the differences between tension and relaxation. That ability is the cornerstone of tension management and should always be your principal focus when trying to relieve tension in any part of your body. If you begin to have trouble doing so, go back to tension as a means of reconditioning yourself to again recognize the difference between the two muscle states.

The following are eight sets of tension/relaxation exercises, one for each muscle group. As you perform each exercise set, you should carry out the movement to its absolute limit before slacking off the muscle completely and resting. After reaching maximum contraction, stay tensed for at least ten seconds in order to get the full impact of what it feels like to become relaxed. Remember, the more tension you place on each muscle group, the greater the subsequent feeling of relaxation will be.

Practice Session #1 — Hands

Tension: With hands at your sides, clench your fists as hard as possible. Keep them clenched for at least ten seconds. At first, you may want to tense only one hand at a time.

Relaxation: Release your hands and let your fingers slowly uncurl and go limp at your sides.

Note: Repeat this exercise three times, remembering to keep your fingers uncurled for at least ten seconds after maximum tension. After three sets, keep your hands and body relaxed and rested for twenty to thirty minutes.

Practice Session #2 — Arms

Tension: Raise your arms and clench your fists very tightly for at least ten second. At first you may want to tense only one arm at a time.

Relaxation: Allow your arms to fall limply to your sides. Your fingers should hang loosely and motionless.

Note: Repeat this exercise three times with maximum tension each time. After three sets, keep your arms very still and limp for twenty to thirty minutes.

Practice Session #3 — Legs

Tension: Push your feet downward as far and as hard as you can for at least ten seconds. The toes of each foot should also be bent down at the same time.

Relaxation: Allow your feet and toes to go limp and to relax. Keep your legs very loose.

Note: Repeat this exercise three times with maximum tension each time. After three sets, keep your legs very still and limp for twenty to thirty minutes. Never cross your legs while doing this exercise.

Practice Session #4 — Abdomen

Tension: Pull in your abdominal muscles as much as you can. Keep them pulled in for at least ten seconds.

Relaxation: Slowly release your abdominal muscles and sit or lie perfectly still.

Note: Repeat this exercise three times with maximum pulling each time. Breathe slowly and allow your abdomen to relax. After three sets, remain rested for twenty to thirty minutes.

Practice Session #5 — Back

Tension: Arch your spine upward as far as you can, until only your head and buttocks are touching the floor or bed. Keep your back arched for at least ten seconds.

Relaxation: Gradually lower your back and let it become heavy and loose.

Note: Repeat this exercise three times. If necessary, place a small pillow underneath your lower back for more comfort. Remain relaxed for twenty to thirty minutes. This particular exercise is best done only in a fully reclined position.

Practice Session #6 — Shoulders

Tension: Shrug your shoulders toward your head as hard as you can for a full ten seconds.

Relaxation: Release and lower your shoulders slowly. Let them rest limply and heavily.

Note: Repeat this exercise three times with maximum tension each time. After three sets, relax your shoulders and sit or lie quietly for twenty to thirty minutes.

Practice Session #7 — Neck

Tension: Push your head backward against a pillow or mattress as hard as you can for a full ten seconds.

Relaxation: Release your head and let it lie quiet and motionless.

Note: Repeat this exercise three times. Instead of pushing your head backward, you also can lift it forward as far as it will go for a full ten seconds before letting it drop back down to relax. After three sets, let your head remain relaxed for twenty to thirty minutes.

Practice Session #8 — Forehead

Tension: Wrinkle your forehead as much as you can and hold it wrinkled for a full ten seconds.

Relaxation: Slowly release the forehead muscles and let your face relax completely.

Note: Repeat this exercise three times. It may be easier to tense the forehead muscles by frowning severely rather than wrinkling. You also can try to alternate wrinkling and frowning. After three sets, keep your face and head relaxed for twenty to thirty minutes.

When using tension/relaxation techniques, we need to follow certain rules and guidelines in order to make relaxation more effective and easier to learn. These are:

1. *Try to set aside a specific time every day to practice, even if it's only a few minutes each day.* The best times to practice are in the evening after a full day of tension or in the morning to help you get relaxed for the start of a day. However, be careful not to do exercises right before going to bed. If you wait until you're too tired, your mind won't be in the proper state to practice and the natural conditioning process won't be as effective.

2. *Always wear loose, comfortable clothing when practicing relaxation techniques.* Remove your shoes, loosen your buttons and make sure you don't have anything around your neck. Also, remove jewelry in order to prevent small distractions from ruining your practice session. Keep your eyes closed during the entire practice session and never cross your arms or your legs.

3. *Try not to practice on a full stomach.* During digestion, more circulating blood than normal is diverted to the gastrointestinal tract and away from muscles and other tissues. Lowered blood

levels in muscles may cause cramps and discomfort during tension. Also, a full stomach will make you feel sluggish and keep you from concentrating as well as you should on the exercises.

4. *Make sure you practice in a room that's quiet, well ventilated, not too well lit and not too hot or cold.* Any physical distraction will decrease the effectiveness of the exercises.

5. *Muscles always should be relaxed slowly and gradually after tension, never abruptly.* This will give you a better feeling of the transition between complete tension and complete relaxation. Let your body movements be smooth and gentle, always flowing with your breath. During tension, never hold your breath— just let it flow naturally.

6. During each practice session, try to relax the muscle groups that you've previously worked on. For example, during practice session three, while relaxing your legs, also relax your hands and arms. After the eighth practice session, you should be able to relax all the muscle groups each time you tense and relax individual muscle groups.

7. *After muscle groups are tensed and relaxed, it may help you to actually visualize them becoming loose and limp—this is called "imaging."* With smooth, rhythmic breathing, imagine your muscles becoming heavier and heavier. See them getting soft and tender. Give special attention to those muscle groups that are particularly difficult to relax completely. Most importantly, don't give up. Some days may be more difficult than others, and it's vital to repeat the tension/relaxation exercises daily at first so that relaxation becomes second nature.

Tension/relaxation is one of the best and most effective ways to learn relaxation, because it conditions us to distinguish immediately between tensed and relaxed muscles. In other words, through repetition, we actually acquire an ability to recognize even small degrees of tension within each individual muscle group.

Like PMR, tension/relaxation has been very useful in treating a variety of illnesses, including hypertension and migraine headaches. As a stress-management tool, it's one of the best ways to train yourself to trigger the relaxation response whenever you feel tense or anxious. With practice, you'll be able to start relaxation at any stage of tension without ever having to contract your muscles at all. Depending on your physical and mental abilities, this may take anywhere from two weeks to two months. When you finally reach that stage, you'll have accomplished your goal of making relaxation a natural and spontaneous habit that becomes stronger and stronger every time you practice.

· Chapter 11 ·

Meditation

Meditation has been used for centuries in many different parts of the world as a means of achieving deep relaxation and peace of mind. Although some meditative exercises use religious words and phrases, meditation itself is not a religious experience, but a tool that utilizes our internal awareness to release tension.

There are four basic elements necessary for achieving deep relaxation through meditation:

1. *A quiet, peaceful environment.* Just like any other stress management exercise that produces relaxation, meditation requires solitude and comfort. Distractions must be avoided completely, perhaps more so than with any other technique, because concentration is the most basic component of meditation.When choosing a place to meditate, make sure you find a location that will be free from distractions for the entire length of your exercise. It may be a quiet room, a peaceful backyard, a church or even the woods. The important thing is to make sure that you won't be distracted in the middle of your meditation.

2. *A decreased muscle tone.* Comfort is critical, because any undue muscle tension will interfere with concentration. The best positions for meditation are the cross-legged, sitting position on a firm pillow, mattress or rug, or a normal sitting position on a straight, comfortable chair with your head, neck and back straight. Other positions, such as fully or semi-reclined, are not as effective with this particular technique, because there's a tendency to become drowsy and fall asleep.

3. *A passive attitude.* This is probably the most important of the

four elements, because successful meditation requires that you not guide or direct your thoughts, but let them go freely and passively.

4. *A mental device.* In order to help concentration and keep distracting thoughts from interfering with meditation, you need to use a constant stimulus to focus on. A mental device is an object to dwell upon such as a sound, a word, a syllable or a phrase that is repeated over and over during the course of the exercise. Because total concentration is one of the more difficult tasks we can encounter, using a mental device, a "mantra," allows us to break distracting thoughts and reach deeper levels of awareness.

:60 SECOND MEDITATIVE TECHNIQUES

The following are various meditative techniques that can be used to trigger the relaxation response. Try them all and then choose the one that best fits your personality and lifestyle. If you're not a religious person, you may not want to use a meditative technique that uses a religious word or phrase. On the other hand, if you are a religious person, meditation may be more effective and meaningful if it does involve a religious word or phrase. Whichever technique you choose, make sure it allows you to concentrate and become relaxed with the least amount of effort and the least number of distractions.

Meditative Exercise #1
Sit quietly in a comfortable position, close your eyes and breathe through your nose. Become aware of your breathing pattern, and as you breathe out say the word "relax" or "one" silently to yourself. Continue doing this for sixty seconds or so. When you finish, sit quietly for several minutes, at first with your eyes closed and gradually with your eyes open. Maintain a relaxed state throughout the exercise and allow relaxation to occur at its own pace.

Meditative Exercise #2
An example of a religious meditation is a repetitive prayer used by Christians as early as the fourteenth century. It's called "The Prayer of the Heart." Sit down alone, in a comfortable position and in total silence. Lower your head, shut your eyes and begin breathing gently and rhythmically while you imagine yourself looking into your own heart. Visualize your heart and as you breathe out say, "Lord Jesus,

have mercy on me" or "God, grant me peace." Keep repeating this phrase each time you breathe out. If you like, you can change the phrase or use any phrase that suits your own personal attitudes and needs.

Meditative Exercise #3

This meditative exercise makes use of a rhythmic sound that you can focus on to time your breathing rate and to enhance concentration. Adjust a metronome to a slow setting, say forty to sixty beats per minute and then begin an even breathing pattern that follows the beat of the metronome. Once your breathing pattern is established and you've begun concentrating on the click of the metronome, say the word "relax" at the same pace as both breathing and clicking. After doing this exercise for several weeks, your brain will automatically associate the metronome's beats with relaxation. Soon, you'll condition yourself to relax instantly, because the metronome will act as a subconscious stimulus or cue that triggers the relaxation response.

Meditative Exercise #4

This meditative technique is also called autosuggestion, because it uses some of the principles of self-induced hypnosis, though to a much lesser extent. Sit comfortably in a chair facing a wall about six to eight feet away. Pick a spot or an object on the wall (or place one there) that's about a foot above eye level. As you stare at the focal point, breathe slowly and rhythmically. Starting with the number ten, begin counting backwards, one number for each exhalation. As you count, continue to concentrate on the focal point and begin to feel your body getting more and more relaxed.

Soon after beginning the exercise, your eyelids will become heavier and start to droop. When that happens, just let them close. While your eyes are closed, continue counting, but visualize the numbers in your mind as you say them silently. When you reach the number one, remain relaxed and let yourself feel free and easy. Remain in that position for ten to twenty minutes. When you're ready to come out, count from one to three. At one, prepare yourself; at two, take a deep breath; at three, open your eyes, stand up and stretch.

Practicing this exercise will condition your brain to associate certain numbers (which act as cues) with certain stages of relaxation. Depending on your own individual pattern, number six may stimulate eye closing, number four may stimulate upper body relaxation, and number one may stimulate compete relaxation. The object of this meditation is to induce the relaxation response by suggesting to ourselves that certain numbers stimulate certain relaxation states.

Meditation can be a very effective tool in stress management because it teaches us to relax and to shift our focus away from stressful thoughts and feelings. As long as we don't overdo it by meditating for hours on end, meditative exercises are safe and pleasurable; they bring balance to our body and peace to our mind. Most of all, they condition us to relax spontaneously by using devices such as sounds and objects as stimuli that trigger the relaxation response. Meditation has been around for centuries, bringing inner peace and tranquility to people of all religions and philosophies. We too can experience that peace and tranquility by using the power of our mind to eliminate the stresses in our body.

· Chapter 12 ·

Imaging Techniques
and Self-healing

Imaging—also known as visualization or imaginal relaxation—makes use of mental images as a means of achieving a deeply relaxed state. After meditation, it's probably one of the oldest relaxation techniques practiced by mankind. In this type of exercise, vivid images associated with rest, tranquility and serenity are used as positive feedback messages to the rest of the body. These images act as cues that stimulate the nervous system and cause tense muscles to respond subconsciously by relaxing. Once practiced, imaging can be one of the simplest and most enjoyable of all relaxation techniques. And like other :60 second techniques, it too acts as a tool for triggering the relaxation response—in this case, by conditioning the brain to associate mental images with relaxation.

Imaging also has been used as a method for inducing self-healing. Because of its ability to shift the body's immune system into high gear, imaging has been used successfully to help treat various types of cancers, as well as other diseases linked to a breakdown in the immune response. In combination with radiation or chemotherapy treatments, the use of imaging has resulted in much higher survival rates than with the use of treatments alone. This happens because "natural killer" cells, which are special cells that seek out and attack all types of cancer cells, are stimulated when the body is relaxed. Self-healing is possible when we allow the power of our brain to keep our immune system going at full force during those times when we need it most.

There are many different kinds of imaging exercises. The type of imaging you do will depend on your personality and your past experiences, as well as your likes and dislikes. But regardless of the imaging exercises you choose, you need to follow certain guidelines that will make them much more successful and enjoyable. These are:

1. *Make comfort a priority before starting an exercise.* It's almost impossible to maintain a positive image for any length of time unless you're relaxed and comfortable throughout the imaging session. Any tensions that arise will have a tendency to block or at least affect your concentration and, therefore, disrupt your image.

2. *Make sure that the mental images you choose always fit your own idea of what's truly relaxing to you.* If you hate the beach, for example, you shouldn't use an image of sand and sea as a relaxation device, no matter how relaxing other people think it is. On the other hand, if you find a cool, lush green forest refreshing and relaxing, then use that as a mental image. Always uses an activity, scene or picture that makes you feel the most relaxed and gives you the greatest sense of pleasure and comfort.

3. *Start each imaging exercise with relaxed and smooth breathing.* Imaging is much easier once your mind and body are in the process of becoming relaxed. As you breathe and relax, concentrate on the evenness of your breath first and then begin visualizing. If you have trouble keeping an image in your mind, you may need to reevaluate whether or not your chosen image is indeed the right one for you. There may be something in your image that's causing distraction or discomfort. If another image keeps cropping up in your mind, perhaps from your childhood or from a past vacation, then that particular image may be stronger and more effective than the one you've chosen. With practice, you'll be able to establish an image that's exactly right for you. Therefore, don't ignore images that keep popping into your mind if you find that they make you feel relaxed and peaceful.

4. *Choose images that are vivid, real and meaningful.* Most of us have an idea of what we think the perfect image should be, but in most cases, these fantasy images tend to become blurred and intermittent. The best images come from our own real experiences. Therefore, choose an image that you've experienced and enjoyed, one that has given you pleasure and peace. Because they're part of your stored memory, real images become more vivid and long lasting and will serve you well time and time again.

:60 SECOND IMAGING
EXERCISES USED
FOR RELAXATION

There are literally thousands of examples of imaging exercises, each one as unique as the individual doing it. There are several examples offered here, but put forth with the idea that you'll take the basic outline, change it if you like and incorporate your own "personal image" into it. Although you may want to use one of the exercises given here, you should be aware of your own personal needs and desires in order for this stress management tool to work for you. Remember, it's very important for an image to "fit the individual" and not the other way around.

Imaging Exercise #1

Select a comfortable position, close your eyes and begin breathing slowly and smoothly. With each breath, feel the muscles in your body becoming heavier and heavier. Imagine the tension melting away as you continue breathing rhythmically and naturally. Now picture yourself lying on a warm, tropical beach, basking in the glow of an afternoon sun. Visualize the vivid, beautiful colors of the sky, the earth, the flowers and the plants around you. As you lie on the beach, the warmth of the golden sand penetrates every pore of your body and makes you feel warmer and warmer. The golden sand feels soft and soothing; its warmth enters your hands and feet and begins to creep throughout your entire body. Imagine yourself lying serenely and restfully as your muscles become loose and limp. Feel your body sinking into the sand and drifting deeper and deeper into a state of peace and total relaxation. With each breath, watch your body become more and more relaxed, more and more at peace.

Now feel the warmth of the sunlight all over your body, warming you deeply and gently. Visualize the inside of your body bathed in the golden light, absorbing every ray and glowing as radiantly as the sun. A warm, gentle breeze swirls around your body and warms you even more. Visualize and feel the breeze blowing over every part of your body.

As you visualize these images, it may help to say to yourself: "I feel warm and relaxed," "I feel the warmth spreading throughout my body" or "the warmth of the sand is making my muscles feel so loose and relaxed." Continue the imaging exercise for about twenty minutes or so and then gradually become more alert, saying to yourself three times, "I feel refreshed and relaxed." Slowly open your eyes, take a few deep breaths and stretch for a few seconds.

Imaging Exercise #2

Select a comfortable position, close your eyes and begin a smooth rhythmic breathing pattern. Continue breathing this way for a few minutes and then visualize a picturesque lagoon surrounded by tall palm trees and beautiful flowers. The water is a clear, blue turquoise and overhead is a cloudless sky. You hear nothing but the soft whisper of a breeze as it gently passes over your body and touches your face with its light invisible fingers.

Imagine yourself floating on the calm, gentle water. As you float, the warm water soothes and relaxes your muscles. Feel the water massaging first your feet, then your legs, your arms and finally the rest of your body. The water becomes warmer and warmer and as you drift deeper and deeper into a relaxed state, it begins to melt the tension away. Picture yourself absolutely weightless in the water, perfectly at peace and floating gently, smoothly and slowly. You're one with the water; it surrounds you completely and loosens every muscle in your body. Each time you breathe, the warm, soothing water lifts you slightly. Each time you sink back down, more tension is melted away. Soon, your body is so relaxed in the water that you feel like you're a part of it.

You can do this exercise in a relaxed sitting or lying position or while taking a warm bath. A word of caution when doing this in a bathtub, however. Since this technique will make you feel very relaxed, you may have a tendency to doze off. Make sure your head is propped up with a float or something else that will prevent your head from slipping down into the water. A sudden jolt like that could ruin your next attempt at visualizing. Continue the exercise for about twenty minutes and then visualize yourself slowly floating to shore. Gradually get out of the water, saying to yourself, "I feel so refreshed and relaxed." Open your eyes, stand up slowly and stretch for a few seconds.

IMAGING AND SELF-HEALING

For those of us suffering with illness and disease, the body often is regarded as the enemy. Negative feelings and attitudes are quite common during such trying times, because we tend to start thinking of the body as a source of distress rather than a source of health and pleasure. We develop fears and anxieties, which become worse and worse and lead to ever-spiraling cycles of depression and hopelessness. We give up on ourselves, because we just can't believe that the body that was responsible for the disease in the first place is able to fight it at the same time. Creating positive beliefs through imaging, however, can reverse that cycle of fear and depression. Imaging can actually stimulate our immune system to rise up and fight disease head on!

The benefits of imaginal self-healing result from our positive expectations and attitudes toward illness. Together with traditional medical treatment, which should always be a primary source of therapy, imaging can have a tremendous effect on reversing the disease process, while creating a mental environment that enhances the healing process. In summary, self-healing exercises are effective because they:

1. *Reduce the fear and depression of knowing that our bodies have been taken over by illness.* By regaining a sense of control over the body's immune functions, we develop a more favorable outlook on our health, renew our energy levels and establish a better perspective on life.

2. *Bring about positive physical changes within our immune, endocrine, cardiovascular and nervous systems.* These changes act together to help fight illness and strengthen our ability to resist disease.

3. *Condition our brain to respond to illness and disease in a natural and direct way.* The process of relaxation by itself can decrease stress and tension to the point of completely altering bodily functions so they work for us instead of against us. By using the power of our minds to help fight disease, we enhance our ability to regain and retain health and vitality.

IMAGING AND CANCER TREATMENT

For centuries, doctors have suspected that the mind plays a leading role in the development of cancer. The Greek physician Galen, for example, observed higher rates of breast cancer in women who had melancholy (the early term for depression) than in women who were happy with their lives. Centuries later, a treatise on cancer concluded that individuals who were depressed were more susceptible to cancerous disorders. And by the 1950s, enough scientific studies had been done to show that negative life events have a significant effect on the genesis and development of cancer. Based on one such study involving 250 cancer patients, it was noted that more than half—and in some cases almost 80 percent—of individuals either lost a loved one such as a spouse or child, were not able to express themselves or had very low self-esteem.

In the 1970s, doctors attempted a unique method of cancer treatment, which involved both standard treatment and guided imagery. Patients were instructed to relax deeply while mentally visualizing the cancer being destroyed by their body's own immune system. In numerous cases, cancers that had very low cure rates when treated with radiation or chemotherapy alone were slowed or completely arrested by combining the treatment with imaging.

I have to emphasize, however, that visualization is not meant as a substitute for traditional therapy, but rather as a means to augment or enhance the healing process. Since cancer causes a breakdown in the body's immune response, anything that boosts that immune response can have a positive effect on destroying cancer cells.

There are three important steps in helping treat cancer through visualization. They are:

1. *Achieving a deeply relaxed state.* Imaging works best when your body is at rest. Once you block any stress reactions and evoke the relaxation response, your immune system will be ready to respond as well. Use the meditation techniques discussed earlier as a prelude to visualization.

2. Visualizing the specific cancer within a specific body part. As distasteful as this may seem, it's important to visualize the cancer in order to make it more real and to visualize it being destroyed. It's also important to isolate it within the organ or the system that's being attacked by the cancer cells.

3. *Visualizing the treatment being used successfully to attack the cancer.* It's not very helpful to visualize cancer cells that are not being destroyed. Therefore, finish each session with you as the winner and cancer the loser. It doesn't take long for the brain to become conditioned into making the body respond in a more forceful and positive way.

It's critical to focus on proper breathing and becoming deeply relaxed at the start of each self-healing session. Meditation is a great way to begin a visualization session. The progressive muscles relaxation or tension-relaxation techniques in the previous chapters are also very effective. Any method you choose is fine so long as your body becomes deeply relaxed and tension-free before actually beginning the imaging process.

Once you've achieved relaxation, you can begin visualizing the specific cancer in any way you choose (as a shapeless form, as a cell with projecting fingers, as a cell with teeth, etcetera) or you can look at a picture in a medical textbook and visualize the cancer exactly as it is. You may think of cancer as a group of weak and helpless cells that are normally destroyed by our bodies many times during the course of our lifetimes. Each one of us, remember, is susceptible to and develops some kind of cancer growth, which our immune systems normally dispatch quite easily. It's during our more vulnerable times, however, that we need to help our immune systems fight that cancer growth in new and powerful ways.

Next, picture in your mind the treatment that will attack and destroy those weak cancer cells. If radiation therapy is used, imagine laser beams or spurts of energy hitting the cells and shattering them to pieces. The dead cells are then attacked by an army of strong and aggressive white blood cells, which swallow them up and carry them away from healthy tissue. The normal cells repair the damage and continue to thrive. If the treatment is chemotherapy, imagine the chemical distributing itself among the cancer cells, poisoning them as they come into contact with it. Because the cancer cells are weak and helpless, they are destroyed while the normal healthy cells continue to grow and become healthier.

The best results have been achieved when cancer patients performed these kinds of exercises three times a day for at least fifteen minutes at a time. Repetition leads to brain conditioning, which makes the process spontaneous and more effective. With both radiation and chemotherapy, it's important to visualize the cancer shrinking and responding in a positive way, while at the same time visualizing the healthy cells becoming healthier and healthier.

It also helps to imagine yourself free of pain and full of life, energy and vigor. Rather than focusing on the negative aspects of your illness, focusing on your body healing itself and becoming well again is critical in mobilizing the immune system to trigger the healing process.

CREATING POWERFUL
SELF-HEALING IMAGES

When a study was done with cancer patients who practiced guided imagery, researchers discovered that the patients who used weak or negative images were much less successful than those who used strong, positive images. The mind, in essence, was not effectively conditioned to stimulate the body's self-healing mechanisms. This discovery showed that the image itself is a key element in visualization.

According to Dr. Simonton of the University of Oregon Medical Center, Department of Radiation Oncology, there are certain imagery features that are most effective in treating cancer. These images are effective, because they lead to a strong belief in recovery, which is vital for proper health and well-being. Because the mind-body connection is so important in cancer recovery, it's essential that we use strong and appropriate mental images to guide the body's physiological processes. The elements that create the most effective and powerful self-healing images are:

1. *A strong and powerful treatment.* Most of us tend to think of cancer as a powerful disease that takes over our body during a time of weakness and vulnerability. We need to change that perception of cancer and think of the treatment as clearly stronger and powerful enough to destroy any cancer while, at the same time, thinking of it as something that is good to us. Some cancer patients have gone so far as to personalize their treatment by giving it a name, thus making it seem less frightening.

   The image can be made even stronger if we make a vivid distinction between the treatment and the cancer. Using a bland, neutral color such as gray or light brown for the cancer and a vivid color such as red or yellow for the treatment makes it easier to visualize the treatment as a dominant force that can destroy cancer cells. This is especially useful for children who are suffering with cancer and who need some help with guided imagery. They can draw pictures of the cancer, for example, then use different colored crayons to differentiate the good cells from the bad ones.

2. *Weak and helpless cancer cells.* Rather than thinking of cancer cells as able to grow and multiply, it's important to visualize them as weak and helpless. It might help to imagine cancer cells as soft and fragile, not capable of standing up to the treatment. Never give cancer cells the color black, red or orange. These colors tend to stimulate strong emotions. Instead, give them a color like gray in order to make them appear weak and helpless.

3. *Normal and healthy, non-cancerous cells.* The very nature of many cancer treatments dictates that they will affect both cancerous and non-cancerous cells. Therefore, you need to visualize the normal, non-cancerous cells being strong and healthy enough to recover from any damage done to them by the chemical or radiation. So, while the weak and helpless cancer cells are being destroyed, the strong and healthy non-cancerous cells are quickly being repaired and returned to a normal, healthy condition.

4. *Strong and aggressive white blood cells.* The soldiers of our immune system are the white blood cells and the natural killer (NK) cells. They seek out and destroy foreign bodies that break through our lines of defense. Because they play such an important role in fighting cancer, white blood cells should be visualized as strong, powerful and extremely aggressive. They must overwhelm cancer cells with their vast numbers and destroy them completely. After the white blood cells do their job, the dead cancer cells should be seen being flushed completely out of the body. This act of flushing dead cancer cells is important since many patients have a subconscious fear that even dead cancer cells, if left around long enough, can become menacing once again.

   The most powerful images are ones in which cancer cells are significantly outnumbered and overwhelmed by white blood cells. The image of the white blood cells needs to be as vivid, if not more vivid, than the image of the cancer cells in order to establish the belief in one's mind that the body's defenses are much more potent than the disease. Incorporate well-known images for added realism. Imagine, for instance, immune cells armed with swords, cutting the cancer tissue away from healthy cells. Whatever you choose, make it unique to you so that you can repeat the process over and over again.

5. *A healthy, cancer-free body.* Since an important part of imaging is visualizing the desired final outcome, it's vital to see a positive end result. You need to see yourself as healthy, happy, energized and, most importantly, cancer free. If you have trouble visualizing this, you probably still have doubts about your eventual recovery. Try to see yourself doing all the things you

would normally do at the healthiest time of your life and force yourself to visually engage in happy activities. It's critical to set a goal for yourself in which you expect to regain health and finally overcome your battle with cancer. Take control of your image, be assertive in your positive thinking and express total confidence in your body's ability to heal. This positive image of a successful end result will force you to focus on the healing process and reaffirm the confidence you have that your body will ultimately win out over illness.

The concept behind imaging is that total muscle relaxation and even self-healing are possible through the use of a simple mental tool—in this case an image. This mental tool gives us the power to trigger the relaxation response, maintain health and stimulate the natural healing process within us. Again, we should never use imaging as the sole method of healing or disease therapy. Serious illnesses always should be treated by traditional methods, with relaxation and imaging used as important and beneficial aids in the overall treatment process. Each time you practice imaging, it will become easier to do and much more effective. Within a few weeks, you should be able to achieve deep relaxation and begin vivid imaging within a minute or so of starting an exercise.

The benefits of relaxation and imaging have been so great and the success rate so promising that more and more physicians are beginning to use this combined treatment as a means of enhancing therapy for a variety of illnesses and diseases. Practiced regularly in the comfort of your own home, imaginal relaxation is one of the simplest and most effective ways to relieve stress, maintain good health and keep the immune system in a state of constant alert. As more and more is learned about how we respond to stress and about our body's natural defense system, we begin to discover that our body has an extraordinary power and ability not only to cope with day-to-day events, but to literally heal itself in the process.

· Chapter 13 ·

Nutrition and Stress

STRESS, NUTRITIONAL SUPPLEMENTS AND DISEASE PREVENTION

A common question I hear is "Can vitamins, minerals and herbs prevent diseases?" The answer is a qualified "yes," because vitamins and minerals, which replenish important nutrients lost during normal activities, contribute to the revitalization and proper functioning of our organ systems. When we start to feel better because our systems are functioning properly, we have a better outlook on life. When that happens, our positive attitudes will then translate into a healthy immune system. I say qualified, because the overuse of certain supplements can make us feel worse and can actually cause disease.

Vitamins are organic compounds involved in many bodily functions that participate in an incredible array of biochemical reactions. Minerals are needed for even more bodily functions, from blood formation and muscle contraction to nerve transmission and bone development and growth. During times of stress, we need greater amounts of minerals because the body tends to use them up faster. There's no way we're able to cope with stress or fight disease if the basic elements are not there. The brain can only do so much without help from the rest of the body.

The best source of vitamins we have is food. But since many of us don't eat as well as we should, there's nothing wrong with supplementing diet with a high-potency vitamin and mineral tablet. Individuals taking supplements, however, should be aware of side effects caused by overuse.

There have been numerous theories espousing the benefits of vitamins and many clinical studies done on vitamins and their role in disease prevention. One theory states that aging is the result of wear and tear on the body due to free radicals that are reduced by certain vitamins like C and E. Another theory holds that simply maintaining high levels of vitamins will strengthen immunity, because we feel better and truly believe that we're healthier. It's a "power of positive thinking" scenario, so to speak. If you think it, you will be it.

Results on vitamin research have been mixed, but in general there is agreement that certain vitamins may indeed enhance the immune system and, as a result, prevent diseases such as cancer, stroke and heart disease. Here are the most likely candidates and the foods they are found in:

Vitamin A & Beta-Carotene: cantaloupes, carrots, broccoli, dark green leafy vegetables, peppers, spinach, sweet potatoes, tomatoes, liver, dairy products and fish.

Vitamin B6: bananas, peas, turnip greens, carrots, sweet potatoes, chicken, eggs, liver and fish.

Vitamin B12: liver, milk, eggs, cheese, crab, tuna, lamb, veal, poultry and fish.

Vitamin C: broccoli, green peppers, potatoes, tomatoes, grapes, grapefruit and oranges.

Vitamin E: sweet potatoes, whole wheat bread, shrimp, peanuts, pecans, sunflower seeds and almonds.

Most herbal products and supplements are reasonably safe to use in limited doses. There are many books on the market describing herbs and their effects and a list of some of the best herbs is included later in the chapter.

There are some supplements, however, that we need to avoid as part of our overall prevention programs. The following are herbs and supplements that have been classified as unsafe by the FDA, national pharmacy chains and various poison control centers:

Borage: may cause liver damage.

Calamus: may cause cancer.

Chaparral: contains chemicals that may cause liver damage.

Coltsfoot: banned in some countries, because clinical studies show that it may cause tumors and liver cancer.

Comfrey: banned in some countries, because it is known to cause serious liver damage.

Ephedra: adverse side effects include liver damage, hypertension, stroke, stomach disorders, headache, nervousness and arrhythmia.

Foxglove: toxic to various systems.

Gamma-butyrolacetone: also known as Blue Rhino, it has been linked to seizures and life-threatening reactions.

Germander: may cause liver damage.

Life Root: may cause liver damage.

Lobelia: mimics nicotine; it can cause nausea, vomiting, tachycardia and breathing problems.

Pennyroyal: used in some countries for abortions, it induces uterine muscle contractions.

Pokeweed: toxic to the gastrointestinal system; may cause fatal poisoning.

Sassafras: may cause cancer.

Senna: causes arrhythmia and decreased blood electrolytes.

Yohimbe: raises blood pressure and may cause weakness, fatigue, stomach disorders, paralysis, seizures and death.

DIETS THAT BOOST
ENERGY AND IMMUNITY

An added benefit to eating foods that revitalize us and make us feel better is the psychological effect these feelings have on us. Simply feeling better will strengthen immunity, lower stress and prevent disease. On a subconscious level, we all get the message that feeling good means being healthy.

I've already listed the vitamins that researchers say may help us fight cancer, heart disease and other illnesses. Here are some overall health tips, as well as foods and ways to eat them, that studies have shown will boost your energy levels, maintain your immune system in top working order and keep your brain healthy enough to heal the body when it needs it most.

- **Maintain a balanced diet.** The best advice any diet or self-help book can offer is to eat foods that contain all the daily nutrients one needs. Most of us, because we're neglectful or too busy, aren't as conscientious as we should be. Supplements aren't a perfect substitute, but they do offer a way to ensure that we at least get what we need to stay healthy.

- **Consume enough calories.** It is a mistake to decrease too much the amount of calories we eat, since calories are what give us energy. In essence, just as gasoline fuels the cars we drive, calories are the fuel that drives muscles and gives us the energy we need for daily activities. The number of calories we require

depends on age, weight, gender and how active we are. Not getting enough calories will make us feel fatigued and cause our
bodies to defend themselves against starvation by slowing down
metabolism. The best way to eat is to consume the normal
amount of calories needed and to spread those calories out
throughout the course of a day.

- **Snack smart and in moderation.** Despite what the health
gurus may say, it is not bad to snack, so long as we snack on
something that will benefit our bodies. If food is fuel, occasional snacks are like the high powered additives we add to our
engine. But since not all additives are created equally, we need
to be careful of what we consume. The best high-energy snacks
are bananas, dried fruits, nuts, low-fat yogurt, fig bars, grapes,
oranges, strawberries and whole grain cereals.

- **Don't forget the minerals.** The body needs substantially
more minerals than it does vitamins, because it is the minerals that are involved in building and revitalizing body struc-
tures. Nutritionists will tell you that if you're like most people,
you're probably lacking minerals far more than you are vitamins. Calcium, for example, is important to bone development,
nerve transmission and muscle contraction. Phosphorus is
involved in building high-energy molecules. Potassium, like
calcium, participates in nerve transmission. Magnesium is
involved in nerve transmission and chemical reactions and is
crucial in helping us fight stress. Iron is a main component of
hemoglobin, the molecule that transports oxygen throughout
the body. Zinc combines with hundreds of enzymes, which
then catalyze biochemical reactions. It's easy to ignore these
minerals, because vitamins are what get most of the attention.
By getting proper amounts of minerals, we ensure that our
bodies continually repair, restore and revitalize. So when buying supplements, make sure they include all the essential minerals you need.

- **Eat foods that boost immune function.** A poor diet is one of
the biggest reasons that immunity breaks down, especially
during stress. Certain foods, according to experts, have healing properties. In fact, studies done throughout the world have
shown that regardless of the country of residence, the healthiest populations consume diets that are consistently high in

grains, fruits and vegetables and low in meats and saturated fats. To help fight cancer, heart disease and a variety of other illnesses, load up on these fifteen healing foods: apples, beans, broccoli, cabbage, carrots, cauliflower, fish such as salmon and tuna, garlic, grapes, nuts such as almonds and walnuts, onions, peppers, spinach, oranges and tomatoes.

Try some herbs. In many countries, herbs are commonly used to treat maladies and are prescribed more often than traditional medicines. And though some herbs have not been proven effective and may even be dangerous, a few are now accepted as "immune enhancers" and "energy boosters." The herbs that are thought to do this are:

Astragalus: boosts immunity; effective against respiratory infection.
Echinacea: fights colds and flu; strengthens immunity; helps relieve symptoms of chemotherapy.
Garlic: lowers cholesterol; boosts immunity; fights infections.
Ginseng: combats symptoms of stress; enhances energy levels.
Goldenseal: strengthens the immune system; promotes healing.
Green Tea: helps fight cancer and heart disease.
Saw Palmetto: helps ease symptoms of enlarged prostate; boosts immunity.
Siberian Ginseng: combats symptoms of stress; boosts energy and the immune system.

There are literally hundreds of herbal products available. Some are very effective, others are worthless. Consumers need to follow certain guidelines in order to protect themselves from dangerous or ineffective products. Before buying any of them, here are five rules you should follow:

Rule #1: Only use standardized herbal products. Herbs can vary widely in quality and content. Depending on where and how it is grown and how it is stored before it's prepared and packaged, an herb may have a completely different potency than the exact same herb manufactured by a different company. Always look for a standardized extract; i.e. the active ingredient per given weight. If the package doesn't include standardized information, put it back on the shelf.
Rule #2: Buy from reputable companies. Not all herbs are

created equally and the FDA is not in the business of testing herbs for efficacy and safety. Just as herbal products differ in content and potency due to standardization problems, they also differ greatly in quality. The best way to ensure that you're getting a good product is to buy only the best brands from reputable companies. Get into the habit of reading labels. Look for standardization information and proof that the product you're buying has been scientifically tested. Beware of unbelievable claims and never buy a product advertised as a "miracle cure" or some other outrageous description.

Rule #3: Select herbs for specific conditions. There's no such thing as a general herb to treat all ailments. Therefore, select only those herbal products you need for a specific symptom, such as St. John's Wort for depression, Kava for anxiety or Saw Palmetto for prostate hyperplasia.

Rule #4: Choose the right form. Some of us prefer medicines in tablet or capsule form while others would rather swallow a teaspoon of something. Some herbs are not absorbed as well if they're in tablet form, so it's actually better to use them in teas or juices. On the other hand, herbs like saw palmetto are not water soluble and, therefore, must be taken as tablets. Since a lot of research has been done to determine which herbs are most effective or ineffective in what form, it is one more reason to buy only from reputable companies.

Rule #5: Ask your doctor about possible interactions. Some herbs interact not only with other herbs, but with medicines and foods. If you're taking a prescription medication, always consult your doctor before taking any herbal product. If you notice any negative physiological changes after taking an herb, stop immediately.

One of the things we can do to improve health and maintain strong and balanced mind-body connections is to learn how to read nutrition labels. Since nutrition is a key factor in immune function, mental alertness and disease prevention, what we put into our bodies is critical in how we feel and how healthy we remain.

"Take responsibility for your own health," says Dr. Koop, former Surgeon General of the United States. In other words, we shouldn't depend on anyone else to keep us healthy and free of disease. That task is ours and ours alone, because by the time we see our doctors it's often because we've neglected their advice in the first place. Sometimes it's too late.

Disease prevention is very often a matter of not doing certain things, not eating the wrong foods and not living a certain lifestyle. Eighty-five percent of cancers, for example, can be avoided by not using tobacco or alcohol, not eating foods high in fat and not overexposing ourselves to the sun or toxic chemicals. The same is true for heart disease and other illnesses. If we combine the care we take in not doing things with the proactive, preventive stress-reducing measures throughout this book, we can be assured of a healthy immune system that will protect us throughout life.

WHY STRESS MAKES
US FAT

Weight gain can be caused by a number of factors. Genetic predisposition, a sedentary lifestyle, an abundance of high fat foods and simple overeating are some of the causes that explain why more people today are overweight than ever before. But another factor, easily overlooked, but often a hidden culprit in significant weight gain, is the effect of stress hormones on fat deposition and appetite.

We've already seen how the stress response triggers an avalanche of hormones that affects nearly every system in the body. The principle stress hormone, cortisol, has a dramatic influence on weight gain, because of its effect on insulin, carbohydrate metabolism, satiety and fat cells. When an individual encounters stress, for example, the body's defenses are mobilized and the following series of events occur.

- The brain releases cortisol.

- Cortisol converts glycogen (the stored form of sugar) to glucose for energy and causes adipose tissue to deposit more fat. It also stimulates the appetite centers in the brain and the pancreas to release insulin. Insulin is basically a storage hormone that directs the body to store the nutrients you eat.

- Insulin further stimulates appetite, causes cells to absorb sugar and increases the deposition of fat throughout the body. Excess insulin, therefore, makes us fat not only because it causes us to store fat, but also because it inhibits the breakdown of fat for energy.

- Adipose cells secrete leptin, which then decreases appetite and speeds up metabolism, but which does not work very effectively during stress.

- Increases in cortisol and insulin, together with the body's non-response to leptin increases weight gain and maintains body fat composition.

FOODS THAT COMBAT
STRESS REACTIONS

Foods can have a profound influence on how we feel and, consequently, on how stressed we are and how well we cope. In general, so-called "high-stress" foods are those that contain saturated fats or empty calories, i.e. large amounts of carbohydrates or refined sugar, which cause us to produce high levels of insulin. A sudden increase in insulin not only increases our appetites to the point that we can't control overeating, it disrupts other organ systems and can make us feel lousy. Here are foods that either stress us out or help us combat stress.

Foods To Avoid

Cake, Candy, Cheese, Cold cuts (except for low fat meats such as turkey and chicken breast), Doughnuts, Fried foods, Meats high in saturated fat, White pasta, Sweet rolls, White rice, Whole milk, White bread.

Foods That Fight Stress

Beans, Brown rice, Chicken breast (not fried), Cottage Cheese, Fat free or low fat milk, Fish, Fruit (especially apples, bananas, cantaloupe, oranges and pineapple), Legumes, Nuts, Oatmeal, Soybeans, Sunflower seeds, Turkey breast, Vegetables (especially dark green and those with beta-carotene), Wheat germ, Whole grain cereal, Whole wheat bread.

· Chapter 14 ·

The Mind-Body Connection

What physician at some time has not proclaimed, "This patient doesn't have the will to live," or "It's in God's hands now." In fact, every medical student who spends four years in medical school and then four years in a residency program learns eventually and often reluctantly that there's more to healing than simply prescribing pills and performing surgery.

For some time now, countries throughout the world have been taking that philosophy a step further. They've encouraged physicians to utilize all the tools at their disposal, including natural medicine, and not to rely solely on modern methods that have been sanctioned by organizations like the American Medical Association or the College of Surgeons and Physicians. A few of the world's leading teaching hospitals even offer courses and programs in spirituality and self-healing.

Fortunately, patients searching for something more than traditional doctor-patient interactions are finding that many physicians are beginning to take a more serious view of what has been labeled "alternative medicine." In addition to standard therapy, these physicians are successfully treating their patients by non-traditional means, knowing that a person's mind can often be the most powerful instrument in his or her arsenal against illness and disease.

Recognizing that the mind plays a key role in a variety of health issues, the National Institutes of Health has recently funded five mind-body research centers that will focus on how beliefs, attitudes, values and stress affect physical and mental health. Together with twelve NIH institutes that have agreed to co-sponsor the initiative, the universities of Pittsburgh, Michigan, Wisconsin and Miami, as well as Carnegie Mellon and Ohio State University, have begun major studies to help us understand the mind-body interaction and lead us to more effective approaches for the treatment and prevention of disease.

There are countless examples in medical literature of competent and caring physicians making errors in judgment or giving up on their sick and dying patients only to see them recover miraculously. It's happening much more often than we realize, because people are taking charge and learning to use the restorative power of their own minds and alternative treatments, to assist in their own healing. Sometimes, it's a mystery how these astounding recoveries happen. More often they can be attributed to the fact that our immune systems are directly connected to specific signals from our brains which, after all, are the organs that control our perceptions of everything about us. This chapter offers information that might otherwise be unavailable to people who want to take some control and responsibility for their own health and well-being.

Most individuals have no idea how this could be possible and have a very limited understanding of the connection between the mind and the body. Many are interested to learn that much of this information and these techniques have been around for thousands of years. Some have been squelched by physicians trained from their first year in medical school to stay away from non-traditional medicine, for fear that patients would be less dependent on the medical establishment if they had more control over their own healing. Furthermore, some non-traditional techniques have been demonized by pharmaceutical companies that depend on the billions of dollars generated from patentable, synthetic products.

The mind is truly connected to the rest of the body. The human brain has evolved into an organ so powerful that it either can trigger disease or prevent it. Our goal should be nothing less than to harness even a small fraction of that power, so that we may not only live longer, but much better as well. Hopefully, after reading this book, you will begin to take charge of your body and condition your brain to improve your health.

In recent years, we have made significant advances in the field of mind-body medicine. Studies funded by the National Heart, Lung and Blood Institute have shown that stress-management training can reduce the fear and anxiety associated with asthma, thus reducing asthma attacks. The National Cancer Institute has demonstrated positive effects of psychosocial group therapy for cancer patients, including mood improvement, pain relief and even life extension. In one study, patients with metastatic breast cancer who received weekly group therapy lived an average of eighteen months longer than those who did not participate in the group treatment. Other mind-body studies have shown similar results:

- As many as 30 percent of heart attacks are triggered by external and behavioral factors and interventions like stress management have been shown to reduce morbidity.

- Infant health and survival are enhanced by touch. Studies funded by the National Institute of Child Health and Human Development have also shown that depriving touch results in a decrease of hormones critical for growth and development.
- Personality factors have been linked to mortality in various studies. One characteristic, cynical hostility or lack of trust, was found to predict increased rates of death from all causes in several epidemiological studies, including a twenty-year study of executives, a twenty-five-year study of physicians and a twenty-five-year study of attorneys.
- Scientists as the National Institute of Aging have discovered that participants who as children were socially dependable or conscientious were, as adults, 30 percent less likely to die in a given year than those who scored low on these personality characteristics.
- According to many studies, there is strong evidence supporting the efficacy of relaxation approaches in reducing chronic pain associated with many medical conditions. Patients learning personal mind-control techniques can reduce their pain in various categories, including back, neck, joint and migraine headaches.
- Based on a decade or more of research, behavioral and social treatment and prevention approaches are successful in treating health problems including diabetes, arthritis, gastrointestinal problems, violence, depression and alcohol and drug abuse.

During the past few decades, we've learned more about mind/body interactions and health than we have in all of the previous years combined. Based on all the research and studies undertaken by many different organizations, we've come to the irrefutable conclusion that our beliefs, emotions, behaviors, thoughts, family relationships and even our cultural diversities are just as relevant to our health as our genetic inheritance and physiology.

In other words, the link between mind and body operates at all levels of biology, from our organs to our cells to the very molecules that drive our biochemical reactions and make us the unique human beings we are. As more and more doctors and scientists accept the mind-body connection as a key life force in preventing disease processes, we'll continue to make strides in improving health and well-being. In the end, though, it's really up to us. By taking responsibility for ourselves and by learning to control our biological functions through mental conditioning, we'll guarantee ourselves a lifetime of health and self-healing.

The lessons learned from these studies should be a warning to anyone concerned about the rising cost of health care. Firstly, if a nation wants to become healthier, it needs to pay more attention to the continued high rates of poverty within its minority populations. Secondly, if individuals themselves want to break the cycle of poor health and high mortality rates, they need to take active measures to reduce the stress and depression in their own lives. The best ways to do that are by improving education, which guarantees a better life and is the fastest way out of poverty, by changing lifestyles to one that prevents illness and keeps one healthier throughout life and finally by reversing negative attitudes and perceptions, which can be the single greatest threat to health and well-being.

THE PLACEBO EFFECT

Faith healing, rituals, magic elixirs and herbal concoctions all have one thing in common. They have the power to heal by making use of the most powerful medicine known to man: the placebo. For more than 2,000 years, these unorthodox medical treatments have produced astounding improvements in health that could not be explained in traditional terms. But as we've learned more and more about how the mind and the body operate as a complex unit — one controlling and regulating the other — we're only now beginning to see how.

For most of us, the notion that brainpower alone is enough to cure a disease is hard to accept, but the fact is that individuals often respond dramatically if they think they're being administered a drug and have been given nothing more than a sugar pill. Our belief system gives us more healing power than we realize. If we think we're being treated, if we believe that someone cares enough to listen to our complaints, if we're convinced that our symptoms can be controlled and alleviated and our health improved, our body will shift into defense mode even without medication or surgery.

Today, doctors accept the placebo effect as a powerful physiologic response that, according to one Harvard study, may be responsible for as many as 30 to 50 percent of all successful medical treatments. It helps to explain why saline injections can work as well as analgesics, why sugar pills thought to be drugs can lower blood pressure, cure depression and fight a variety of illnesses and why taking a pill having a color associated with a specific effect will actually produce that very effect.

In many cases, the placebo may be as good or even better than the actual treatment. Dr. Irving Kirsch, a professor of psychology at the University of Connecticut, for example, found that placebos perform as well as antidepressants, including Prozac, in 75 percent of all patients treated. It has also been shown that multicolored placebo pills work best overall, green placebos produce better results in anxious or phobic patients, red or orange ones perform better as stimulants, blue ones as sedatives and yellow ones for depression. Nothing on the drug market today can hold a candle to the power and versatility of our mind's own naturally produced chemicals.

Placebos, amazingly, are also organ-specific. They work exactly the way the actual drug is supposed to work on precisely the body part or organ they're intended to affect. So a placebo taken for an ulcer will heal the ulcer, one taken for headaches will blunt pain in one's head and one that a patient believes will work against arthritis will improve joint mobility.

To illustrate this, a group of patients was told they were being given medication that would trigger pronounced stomach activity. Shortly after taking the placebo, two-thirds of the subjects experienced strong stomach churning. Their belief in the medication actually caused the physical response. Other studies done on patients suffering from heart disease, arthritis and skin disorders have demonstrated similar results, which may explain why so many useless drugs and health products work on people who truly believe they can be cured of their ailment by taking a pill. Even herbal products that have never been clinically proven to work can improve health simply by making one think they can. It's not the drug or the herb, but the brain that is responsible for the physiological response.

Surgery can elicit the placebo effect even more dramatically. In a famous hospital study done in 1958, researchers wanted to see if heart patients with poor circulation and angina would respond to "sham surgery," in which physicians made small skin incisions in order to mimic the real operation. Following surgery, the sham-operated patients improved better and recovered faster than the patients who actually had surgery. In a more recent pilot study involving veterans who'd undergone sham knee operations, the results were so positive that doctors are now testing this sham procedure on as many as 200 patients.

How does this happen? And how exactly do the chemical signals produced during a placebo response trigger a healing process that can be more effective than any medicine we take? The answer lies in our own subconscious abilities to tap into an inner pharmacy that has at its disposal virtually everything needed to bring our bodies back into homeostasis. Working together with the nervous, endocrine and immune systems, the staggering array of biochemicals we have in that inner pharmacy is what sets the healing process in motion.

So why doesn't this work for everyone? Why are some patients so quick to heal while others languish? Typically, patients having the greatest placebo effects are those who participate actively in their own healing. They adhere to directions, have positive attitudes, practice stress management, follow rules and guidelines and are confident that their illness will be treated successfully. On the other hand, negative thoughts and attitudes and a belief that there's no hope produce what has been coined the "nocebo effect," a negative reaction that works to depress the immune system. Which proves one thing: that something within those of us who have positive attitudes and the will to get better will cause the brain to produce the chemicals necessary to trigger spontaneous healing.

If we strip ourselves down to what we're composed of — a complex system of molecules, chemicals and nerve connections that interact and respond to our mental suggestions — it makes sense that the placebo effect is really nothing more than a normal immune response. How else can we explain what some people call "miracle cures," but what more and more doctors refer to as unexplained spontaneous healing? Mind over matter is not simply a catch phrase. It is a truth that is based on what we know to be fact: the brain, given the right set of directions, the right environment and the proper stimuli, will always choose healing over disease.

SPONTANEOUS HEALING: COINCIDENCE OR A FACT OF BIOLOGY?

Why don't we hear more about the cancer patient who is given six months to live, but is still alive six years later? Or about a tumor that doesn't respond to chemotherapy, yet begins to shrink after the patient decides to use imaging and other alternative therapies to treat himself? Part of the answer may be ignorance, but much of it has to do with arrogance on the part of the medical establishment and the fear of ridicule by editors of major medical journals.

After spending four years as a researcher at a medical school and teaching hospital, I learned that doctors, while they may think of themselves as scientists, are sometimes narrow-minded when it comes to non-traditional methods of healing. Journal editors are usually physicians who work at these medical schools or at research hospitals and who view with skepticism anything that cannot be measured by rigid experimental standards. What they allow in print are papers and abstracts that conform to exact standards of science filled with statistics, graphs, charts and double-blind studies, all designed to prove or disprove everything. What's missing from these important sources of medical information is what may really be going on in such unexplained. We should be trying our hardest to learn everything we can about this phenomenon.

Until recently, medical researchers who tried to submit articles about an unexplained, spontaneous healing to major journals had better odds of winning the lottery than having their study published. It's still difficult for scientists to accept or confirm what cannot be tested or proven. Self-healing, in many cases, can't be explained to anyone's satisfaction. And that's precisely why individuals looking for facts about self-healing are often forced to go elsewhere for advice and information.

A physician friend of mine had told me that 85 percent of the patients that walk through his office every day cure themselves. Most doctors can't accept that, because it makes them feel less significant. But simply put, spontaneous healing occurs because something inside of us can cause a major response in our immune system. The dozen or so types of white blood cells produced by our lymphatic system, spleen and thymus, rather than be suppressed, literally flood our body and attack everything that is foreign and causes illness.

We shouldn't be surprised at all that this happens so often. If it didn't, we would get diseases constantly and die at rates that would quickly wipe out the human population. What should surprise us is that we aren't being told that immunity can be strengthened significantly through brain conditioning and that one of the greatest facts of biology is that the body very often heals itself without our even knowing it

THE STRESS-CANCER
CONNECTION

Cancer is not a single disease, but many. And just like there is no single cause or factor that triggers cancer growth, there is not a single, universal treatment that will cure it. Regardless of what type of therapy is used, however, patients can improve the effectiveness of whatever treatment method they are undergoing by utilizing certain techniques such as imaging, which can stimulate the immune system and aid in the healing process.

The term cancer is used to categorize any kind of malignant tumor growth. Normal cells have a defined life span, roughly a few weeks to a few months. When control of cell division is lost, the cell may go on dividing indefinitely. In other words it becomes immortal. The dividing cells proliferate, destroying adjacent tissues and taking away the nutrients that normal cells need to live and reproduce.

One of the defining characteristics of many cancer cells is that they lose their ability to stay anchored to tissue. When tumor cells break loose from their home tissue, they travel through the blood and lymph and invade other areas of the body, where the process continues and new masses form. Unless the process is stopped, the cancer cells simply take over and ravage the tissues to which they travel.

A new experimental treatment called antiangiogenesis involves drugs that literally cut off the blood supply to cancer cells and essentially starve the tumor. Researchers have discovered that a protein is responsible for blood vessel growth in tumors and they believe that drugs can eventually be developed to block that protein and specifically target tumor cells.

The two main factors that cause tumor development and growth are genetics and the environment (natural and man-made chemicals, toxins, etc.). As many as 25 percent of all people develop cancer at some time in their lives. Next to heart disease, more people will die of cancer than any other disease. In reality, though, we don't know how many of us will actually develop cancer because, more often than not, it's eliminated from our system before we even know it.

As one immunologist once told me, "If the fight is between a cancer cell and a healthy immune system, the immune system usually wins." The problem in many cancer cases is that the immune system is not able to keep up, in which event the cancer wins.

Very few cancers are inherited. Exceptions are some types of leukemia, breast cancer and colon cancer. Some cancers are the result of an interaction between genes and the environment, but most (as many as 80 percent) are the result of factors in the environment such as toxins, foods high in fat and/or low in fiber, industrial chemicals, pesticides, radiation sources, hazardous waste and cigarette smoke. In many cases, a single chemical may not be harmful, but a combination of two or more chemicals may produce an effect a hundred or more times that of an individual chemical alone.

Eliminating these factors from our lives will go a long way to eliminating the risk of getting cancer. In fact, one leading cancer specialist has claimed that most people would not get cancer at all if they simply followed four rules:

1. Don't smoke
2. Avoid chemicals in the environment and in foods
3. Avoid UV radiation from the sun
4. Eat a low fat, high fiber diet

There is one other risk factor that the cancer specialist failed to mention, but which research has shown to be critical in helping the body fight cancer. That factor is emotional well-being and the manner in which a person perceives and responds to stressful events in his or her life. Evidence from clinical research has shown that cancer patients who use positive reinforcement and the power of their minds to help them overcome their illness are much more successful.

Almost every hospital now offers cancer patients ongoing counseling, social support, visualization therapy and stress management. Many are beginning to offer hypnosis as well. These techniques have been shown to extend life span, improve the quality of life and, in some cases, actually cure cancer when other, more conventional treatments have failed.

In the event that someone does get cancer, the goal in any method of treatment is to eliminate the tumor or at least to decrease its size. Modern methods for doing so are surgery, chemotherapy and radiation. Surgery is most effective when the tumor has been detected early and has not spread (metastasized). Chemotherapy and radiation are used to kill metastatic cells that may have spread to other parts of the body. Surgery can be used along with the other methods to ensure that the entire tumor is eliminated in the event that it has spread.

One of the problems with chemotherapy and radiation is that healthy tissue is damaged along with the cancerous cells. If some of the healthy cells happen to be white blood cells, the immune system becomes depressed and infections and other diseases occur. When high doses of chemicals are required, as is the case when cancer has spread throughout the body, a bone marrow transplant is often necessary following chemotherapy, because the drug literally destroys the lymphocytes within the existing bone marrow.

A further problem with all current chemotherapy is that cancer cells may develop resistance to the drug. When that occurs, a cocktail of drugs or stronger drugs need to be administered, but these can cause more extensive damage to healthy tissue.

The best way to beat most cancers is to avoid the risk factors that trigger cancer growth in the first place. Naturally, we can't do anything about the genetic component, but we can at least minimize our potential for developing tumors. Maintaining a steady, healthy immune system is one of the best ways to do that. Stress management, behavior modification, meditation and relaxation techniques all help to maintain homeostasis and bring us back to a state of equilibrium. The techniques found in earlier chapters will help you learn how to do that.

Another way to beat cancer is by knowing your own body. Looking for signs of change and noticing warning signals will help you detect cancer early and help ensure recovery. The odds increase dramatically with early detection. As we saw in chapter 2, one of the best ways to self-diagnose disease while it's in early stages is by recognizing signs and symptoms.

Cancer, for many individuals, needn't be a death sentence. More people recover from cancer than don't and survival rates for many cancers are improving significantly. What we are now beginning to learn, from both research and survivors, is that even a disease like cancer can be overcome much more easily when we use the power of our mind to help fight it.

IS THERE A CANCER-PRONE PERSONALITY?

The results are not yet conclusive, but recent studies have shown that a cancer-prone type of personality may exist. Keep in mind that any negative emotion—depression, hate, sadness or anger, for example—is going to make us more prone to illness and disease. And as we've seen, positive attitudes and perceptions, feelings of gratification, love and especially hope will invariably boost the immune system and protect us from disease.

It's a well-known fact that when patients give up, their odds of beating cancer drop precipitously. Conversely, study after study shows that a positive attitude and a feeling that one is going to win the battle over disease boosts the immune system significantly. The result: survival rates go up even in cancers that are difficult to treat.

According to psychologists, there are two basic personality types that are either more susceptible to cancer or able to battle it more successfully. They are:

Cancer-prone
- tends to repress anger and other emotions
- harbors feelings of resentment and/or hostility
- has a low self-esteem
- unable to cope well with life changes
- thinks negatively and/or pessimistically
- tends to become depressed or have feelings of hopelessness
- focuses too much on the negative aspects of job, family, etc.
- has few friends or no social support network

Cancer-resistant
- manages stress effectively
- controls anger, but expresses positive emotions
- has a sense of hope and optimism
- has a feeling of control over his or her life
- thinks well of him or herself
- maintains a healthy lifestyle, including physical checkups
- stays active and maintains a good social network

These are not hard and fast characteristics. Cancer victims may be happy and optimistic people who rarely get angry and who cope well with change. Some curmudgeons, on the other hand, may never get cancer and live to be one hundred years old. The difference comes into play, according to experts, in how well these people recover if or when they do get cancer. In the event that a cancer is terminal, patients with cancer-resistant personalities tend to live longer and better.

MIND-BODY MEDICINE
AND CANCER

Evidence from various studies points to the fact that mind-body techniques such as hypnosis, massage, guided imagery, social support, psychotherapy, acupuncture, yoga and relaxation can positively affect the outcome of cancer treatment. The studies show the extent to which patients' coping styles and strategies determine medical outcomes and how mortality is reduced for those who have a social support network compared with those who are socially isolated. In addition, it has been established that men do better if they are married and women when they have female friends.

In randomized studies of support groups done at Stanford University, researchers found social interaction and support to be highly successful. One such project with patients who had metastatic breast cancer showed that women who belonged to support groups not only reported a higher quality of life and less pain, but lived with their advanced cancer almost two years longer than non-group therapy patients. This was true even for the anxious and depressed patients in the therapy group.

The conclusion we can draw from these kinds of results is that support acts as a stress buffer. When stress is reduced, the brain is better able to regulate physiological mechanisms, hormone levels and immune function. In the Stanford studies, for example, patients with indications of acute or chronic stress had shorter survival times and poorer quality of life, while patients who felt that their social support was good or had more cohesive family environments had lower stress levels and higher survival rates. Not surprisingly, suppression of emotions caused higher levels of stress.

If there's one lesson that cancer patients can take from all this mounting evidence, it's that working the mental side of one's mind-body connection is key to better recovery or, at the very least, a longer life. Today, some patients spend more on alternatives than they do on primary care, a demonstration of how motivated people are to find solutions to their cancers. We need to be wary of wasting our time and money on treatments that don't work or that steer us away from helpful, proven therapies. We also need to recognize that traditional medicine may not be enough and that mind-body medicine may be just what we need to help get us through.

THE STRESS OF CANCER
TREATMENT

"The cure is worse than the disease" is a common expression cancer patients know all too well. Two problems patients face in their recovery are the side effects of chemotherapy treatment and the negative stress reactions that ensue and consequently lead to physical reactions, negative attitudes, depressed immune function and poor therapy results. A friend of mine who had a rare type of cancer and was undergoing chemotherapy once told me that his treatment was so bad that he felt like just giving up. To him, it seemed as if the treatment was making his disease even worse.

Overcoming the physical and emotional stress of treatment is an arduous task, but those who persevere tend to recover more quickly and have fewer remissions down the road. Conversely, those who give up or who don't utilize stress management strategies during and after treatment are often the ones who succumb the most rapidly.

It's important to remember that any kind of stress triggers the release of cortisol. Cortisol, in turn, depresses the immune system and blocks the production of both NK and white blood cells. Patients who are suffering from the physical side effects of chemotherapy and the emotional stress of having cancer will invariably have even more lowered immune responses.

There are several things patients can do if they are having severe physical or emotional side effects. Relaxation exercises, imaging, meditation, breathing techniques and other stress management strategies will go a long way in helping combat negative stress reactions and boosting energy levels. The suggestions throughout this book can help alleviate many symptoms.

STRESS AND HIV

HIV, or human immunodeficiency virus, is a retrovirus that binds to receptors found on membranes of immune system T cells. When HIV attacks a cell, the virus is internalized, copied into DNA, then migrates into the nucleus where it inserts itself as part of the host DNA. In many cases, the inserted viral genes remain dormant, sometimes for as long as ten or more years. AIDS, or Acquired Immune Deficiency Syndrome, is a collection of twenty-six clinical conditions (the most common are Kaposi's sarcoma and lymphomas) that are the result of prolonged HIV infection.

Once a person is infected with HIV, the immune cells begin to lose normal function. Antibodies are produced in response and other T lymphocytes form to help fight off infection. Shortly thereafter, a period of latency ensues in which there are no symptoms and, depending on the health and lifestyle of the patient, the course of infection may last for years. During this time, billions of T cells are infected and destroyed, but half are replaced. Half the virus particles are also destroyed.

The immune system continues to destroy HIV and replace T cells until the body begins to lose its uphill battle. Eventually, so much virus is produced that the immune system can no longer keep up. When this happens, T cell counts begin to decrease from a normal of 600-1200/uL to less than 200/uL. At this stage, the individual becomes susceptible to myriad illnesses and major diseases. Stress, according to current research, can increase severity of infectious viruses such as mononucleosis and can activate dormant viruses such as genital herpes, cold sores and HIV. Studies have shown, for example, that chronic depression and negative attitudes were associated with a rapid decline of T cells, but levels of NK cells increased in those with positive attitudes. Another study found that subjects who actively fought their disease and were able to cope well with the stress of having HIV significantly prolonged their progression from stages II and III to stage IV.

According to Dr. Neil Schneiderman of the University of Miami, HIV-infected men are at great risk for developing psychological and physical health problems because of the stress they're under. Based on studies he has done since the mid-1980s, he has concluded that stress management significantly lessens the impact of the disease by diminishing HIV-related complications and the reoccurrence of other opportunistic viral infections.

AZT was the first drug used to treat HIV infection. There has been some debate about its effectiveness, especially because the side effects are often so terrible. It has been replaced by more powerful treatments like protease inhibitors, but it's typical for powerful drugs to have even greater side effects. And with greater side effects come greater stress reactions and the risk of illness and disease that is not even related to the infection.

Currently, there are two problems with the new class of drugs used to treat HIV, including protease inhibitors. Firstly, many patients suffer worse physical side effects that they did with AZT, which adds to the emotional stress associated with the disease. In some cases, patients are actually regressing, because the stress of treatment is causing them to get sick earlier than they would have without treatment. This also makes it difficult to keep HIV-infected patients on the strict regimen required for the drug to be as effective as it can be.

Secondly, new, more virulent strains of HIV are beginning to emerge, which are resistant to drugs that were effective only a few years ago. Resistance and mutation increase even more quickly when patients aren't absolutely committed to taking their medications regularly. So, today, despite new and more powerful drugs and a decline in mortality rates, it's more critical than ever for patients to use all the means they can to help alleviate the stress associated with HIV and its treatment.

One team of researchers believes it may have discovered one of the ways in which stress causes the progression of HIV and AIDS. They found that prolactin and growth hormone, both of which are released during stress reactions, could promote retroviral production, because of their effect on virus-producing cells. Individuals who are depressed, who cannot cope well with life events, who are physically challenged and whose lifestyles contribute to daily stress are the ones most prone to immune system breakdown, falling T cell counts and rapid progression of the disease.

In light of these findings, doctors are now treating patients both physically and psychologically. They have seen how rapidly a patient can deteriorate, even when he or she is faithful in taking medications, and they now know that the body will take its cues — both positive and negative — from the mind. In the fight against a disease like AIDS, the connection between mind and body can make the difference between dying from AIDS or living long enough to see a cure or a better treatment.

The correlation between the mind and specifically between stress and immunity is only now beginning to be appreciated. A recent NIH conference presented paper after paper showing the link between mind and body and between the mind and a person's ability to fight off disease. More scientists than ever are recognizing what was once dismissed: the power one has to heal the body through mind control.

When it comes to stress, how do we know that it's actually the stress and not something else that's causing many of our health problems? The evidence that stress is a root cause of disease is also mounting. In many parts of the world, where stress is not a normal part of life, coronary heart disease is rare. Once these people are exposed to the stresses of modern society, they become as susceptible as everyone else. Other studies also show conclusively that cholesterol levels, hypertension, diabetes and other illnesses increase with stress. In one study of nine-to sixteen-year-olds, for example, it was discovered that even a routine act of reading out loud in front of classmates caused significant elevations in blood pressure.

Until recently, most illnesses were attributed to diet, heredity, lifestyle and environment. Evidence now points to stress and the mind-body connection as a major factor in a wide range of illnesses from headaches to ulcers to cancer. Many of these illnesses can be prevented or controlled by learning to use techniques and behavioral changes that trigger the healing power of the mind-body connection. Managing the stress in our lives is, without a doubt, one of the single most important elements in ensuring that our immune system is there and ready for us when we need it most.

· PART III ·

SELF-HELP STRESS TESTS AND EVALUATIONS

· Chapter 15 ·

Testing Your
Stress Knowledge

How much more do you know about stress and how it affects you? The following stress tests are meant to make you more aware of stress and coping strategies and make you more aware of stress management as a tool for better living. If you answer a question incorrectly, go back to the section of the book that deals with that aspect of stress and read it once again. It's important to review those areas that you're unsure of in order to make stress management a complete and effective method for relieving the stress and anxiety in your life. If you answer all or most of the questions correctly, you can take heart in the fact that you're now your own stress expert and are well on your way to becoming healthier and stress-free.

FACTS ABOUT STRESS

	TRUE	FALSE
1. People react to emotional stress just as easily as they do to physical stress.	_____	_____
2. Constant arousal due to stress can cause a person's blood pressure to remain low.	_____	_____
3. Stress due to overload can result from demands that occur at home.	_____	_____

4. An individual who is adjusting to   _____   _____
   many life changes in a short period
   of time is less likely than usual to
   become ill.

5. Thinking about an unpleasant   _____   _____
   event is never as stressful as
   actually experiencing that event.

6. Thinking of oneself as useless   _____   _____
   and powerless can increase one's
   stress level.

7. The most stressful situations are   _____   _____
   usually those over which people feel
   they have a great deal of control.

8. Stress may decrease the body's   _____   _____
   ability to defend itself against disease.

9. Severe stress may cause people to   _____   _____
   have accidents.

10. People who have Type A personalities   _____   _____
    are more likely to suffer from stress
    reactions.

11. One of the most common traits of   _____   _____
    Type A personality is doing only one
    thing at a time.

12. Excessive stress affects the body's   _____   _____
    ability to utilize nutrients such as
    vitamins and minerals.

13. A person under stress may feel   _____   _____
    confused.

14. Overload occurs when people are   _____   _____
    able to meet the demands which are
    placed on them.

15. A person under stress is usually
   able to perform tasks better than usual.   _____   _____

16. Some degree of stress is necessary
   for life.   _____   _____

17. Stress disorders are caused by
   constant stress arousal, leading
   to organ system failure.   _____   _____

18. Too much stimulation is always
   more stressful than too little.   _____   _____

19. The stress produced by a situation
   depends more on the situation than
   on the person's perception of the
   situation.   _____   _____

20. The Type A personality is associated
   with heart disease.   _____   _____

21. The best level of stress is that amount
   which improves a person's performance
   without producing harmful side effects.   _____   _____

22. Frustration occurs when individuals lack   _____   _____
   the ability to take necessary actions
   or when their actions are blocked by
   external obstacles.

23. Favorable life changes are never as
   stressful as unfavorable life changes.   _____   _____

24. The amount of stress individuals feel
   when in a crowd depends on how
   much control they think they have in
   the situation and on their cultural
   background.   _____   _____

25. An individual's reaction to stressors
   is determined by his or her prior
   attitudes, experiences, values and
   even religion.   _____   _____

26. Thinking of one's self as helpless and   _____   _____
    worthless can lead to increased stress.

27. An individual's expectation about   _____   _____
    a stressful event can influence
    his or her stress level significantly.

28. Physiological responses to stressors   _____   _____
    occur automatically, without very
    much conscious thought.

29. Hormones released under stress   _____
    remain in the body for only a short
    period of time.

30. Arthritis and cancer may be   _____   _____
    indirectly related to stress.

31. A person under stress usually   _____   _____
    doesn't return to old habits if they're
    inappropriate to the present
    situation.

32. An individual's stress level can   _____   _____
    increase if he or she receives
    no information or false information
    about a potentially stressful event
    prior to its occurrence.

33. During prolonged stress, the body   _____   _____
    enters a phase in which everything
    returns to a normal level of functioning
    without any symptoms of stress.

34. Mental health problems, such as   _____   _____
    depression, should never be treated
    as emotional stress responses.

35. There is no evidence that stress   _____   _____
    causes an acceleration of the aging
    process.

36. Many cases of sexual dysfunction,   _____   _____
    such as impotence, disinterest in
    sex and premature ejaculation are
    a direct result of stress.

37. The body can be conditioned to relax   _____   _____
    just as quickly and easily as it's
    conditioned to tense up during stress.

38. One of the biggest sources of stress   _____   _____
    is the inability to make use of time.

39. Diet and nutrition are not very   _____   _____
    important factors in stress reactions.

40. Muscles that are constantly   _____   _____
    contracted lead to increased anxiety
    and emotional stress.

Scoring Key:

(1) **T**	(2) **F**	(3) **T**	(4) **F**	(5) **F**	(6) **T**	(7) **F**
(8) **T**	(9) **T**	(10) **T**	(11) **F**	(12) **T**	(13) **T**	(14) **F**
(15) **F**	(16) **T**	(17) **T**	(18) **F**	(19) **F**	(20) **T**	(21) **T**
(22) **T**	(23) **F**	(24) **T**	(25) **T**	(26) **T**	(27) **T**	(28) **T**
(29) **F**	(30) **T**	(31) **F**	(32) **T**	(33) **T**	(34) **F**	(35) **F**
(36) **T**	(37) **T**	(38) **T**	(39) **F**	(40) **T**		

Total Number Correct _____   35—40   = Excellent
                                      30—34   = Good
                                      25—29   = Fair
                                      Less than 25   = Poor

COPING WITH STRESS

	TRUE	FALSE
1. Imagining heaviness and warmth in one's body parts is an effective relaxation technique.	_____	_____
2. An individual should consume more caffeine during stressful times.	_____	_____
3. Competitive physical activity is an effective stress management strategy.	_____	_____
4. Involvement in the pleasure of physical activity leads to feelings of well-being.	_____	_____
5. Breaking down complicated tasks into smaller parts can reduce stress.	_____	_____
6. Stress can be reduced by avoiding routines whenever possible.	_____	_____
7. When undergoing important life changes, stress can be reduced by increasing the number of other changes that are made.	_____	_____
8. Heartbeat rate can be monitored through biofeedback.	_____	_____
9. Individuals should not try to change their relation to stressors.	_____	_____
10. Sitting comfortably helps to quiet one's internal environment.	_____	_____
11. Progressive muscle relaxation is an effective technique for relieving such illnesses as hypertension and ulcers.	_____	_____

12. Anticipating periods of boredom
and planning activities for those
periods can reduce stress.

_____   _____

13. When using physical exercise as a
stress management technique, one
should try to exert oneself as much
as possible.

_____   _____

14. In muscle relaxation exercises, an
individual attempts to eliminate the
physical sensations that are
associated with relaxation.

_____   _____

15. Becoming less competitive with
one's self and others is an effective way
to reduce Type A behavior.

_____   _____

16. Delegating authority and responsibility
to others will have no effect on stress.

_____   _____

17. To be effective, relaxation must be
used at the same time and place each
time it's done.

_____   _____

18. Being in a place away from other
people helps to quiet one's internal
environment.

_____   _____

19. Focusing on one's positive
characteristics improves
self-image and reduces stress.

_____   _____

20. Increased muscle activity is a
characteristic of relaxation.

_____   _____

21. Individuals shouldn't try to identify
the environmental situations that
prompt their stress.

_____   _____

22. Even if individuals can't change the
nature of stressors, they can change
their relation to stressors.

_____   _____

23. An effective way to reduce stress is   _____   _____
to find alternatives for goals and
behaviors that one has been unable
to accomplish.

24. Listing tasks in order of their   _____   _____
importance, so that the most
important tasks can be completed
first, helps to reduce stress.

25. Accepting the fact that no one can   _____   _____
do everything perfectly helps to reduce
stress.

26. Vacations, even when they involve   _____   _____
changes in location, routine or level
of stimulation, are always a good
way to relieve stress.

27. Effective relaxation can be achieved   _____   _____
only when used regularly and in long
spurts.

28. Physical activity that is vigorous   _____   _____
enough to bring relaxation afterwards
makes a person less open to the
negative effects of stress.

29. People should learn exactly what   _____   _____
types of situations cause them to
feel stress.

30. During relaxation, it's impossible to   _____   _____
feel nervous or anxious.

31. Relaxation occurs when a person   _____   _____
lets it happen instead of forcing it
to happen.

32. Stress cannot be reduced by   _____   _____
anticipating periods of boredom and
planning something stimulating to
do during those periods.

33. Stress cannot be reduced by establishing routines that become automatic. _____ _____

34. Intentionally changing the stressful aspects of one's life can help one cope with many kinds of stressors. _____ _____

35. Developing close friendships with people one can trust reduces stress. _____ _____

36. One of the best ways to reduce emotional stress is through social support networks. _____ _____

37. Older people can reduce stress by owning a pet. _____ _____

38. Relaxation training allows people to regulate bodily processes that they thought were beyond conscious control. _____ _____

39. People who have difficult things to do increase their stress by setting time aside for breaks. _____ _____

40. Sometimes the best way for individuals to decrease their stress is to avoid places or situations where they feel stress. _____ _____

Scoring Key:

(1)	**T**	(2)	**F**	(3)	**F**	(4)	**T**	(5)	**T**	(6)	**F**	(7)	**F**
(8)	**T**	(9)	**F**	(10)	**T**	(11)	**T**	(12)	**T**	(13)	**F**	(14)	**F**
(15)	**T**	(16)	**F**	(17)	**F**	(18)	**T**	(19)	**T**	(20)	**F**	(21)	**F**
(22)	**T**	(23)	**T**	(24)	**T**	(25)	**T**	(26)	**F**	(27)	**F**	(28)	**T**
(29)	**T**	(30)	**T**	(31)	**T**	(32)	**F**	(33)	**F**	(34)	**T**	(35)	**T**
(36)	**T**	(37)	**T**	(38)	**T**	(39)	**F**	(40)	**T**				

Total Number Correct _____

35—40	= Excellent
30—34	= Good
25—29	= Fair
Less than 25	= Poor

RESPONSES TO STRESS

1. Valerie has just been promoted to a new job in a different city. An appropriate way for Valerie to reduce her stress would be:
   A. Change her hairstyle and way of dressing to reflect her new image.
   B. Take on as much work as she can to keep herself busy.
   C. Establish a suitable schedule soon after she arrives.
   D. Avoid responsibility as much as possible at first.

2. John is in a noisy office and is trying to concentrate on his work. An appropriate way for John to reduce his stress would be to:
   A. Skip lunch and work during lunch hour when the office is quieter.
   B. Rearrange the books and papers on his desk.
   C. Wear more comfortable clothes to work.
   D. Take periodic breaks away from the office to get some relief.

3. David is worried that he will fail his history test, even though he has studied hard for it. An appropriate way for David to reduce his stress would be to:
   A. Stay up late the night before the test in order to study more.
   B. Think about how angry his parents will be if he fails the test.
   C. Go out and take a bicycle ride.
   D. Get up early the next morning and study some more.

4. Arthur is very busy typing when a coworker asks him to help with her typing. An appropriate way for Arthur to reduce his stress would be to:
   A. Help her with her typing, but explain that he won't do it again.
   B. Explain that he can't do her typing and concentrate on finishing his own work.
   C. Pretend that his co-worker's request doesn't bother him and continue working.
   D. Tell his co-worker that he'll do her typing after he's finished with his.

5. David has been told there is no chance that he can pitch for his baseball team, because the manager's brother will be taking his place. An appropriate way for David to reduce his stress would be to:
   A. Look into pitching for another team.

    B. Get to know the other members of the team better.

    C. Tell the owner that he insists on being able to pitch for the team, no matter what.

    D. Quit pitching altogether.

6. Kathy drives home on a busy, crowded freeway. An appropriate way for Kathy to reduce her stress would be to:

    A. Drive with her car windows open slightly.

    B. Make sure that she takes the same route home whenever possible.

    C. Drink a cup of coffee as she drives.

    D. Try an alternate route or a different time when it's not as crowded.

7. Gary is concerned that the quality of his work is not good enough, even though all of the people he works with tell him he's doing a good job. An appropriate way for Gary to reduce his stress would be to:

    A. Spend more time working to improve the quality of his work.

    B. Plan to have a few beers with his coworkers every day after work.

    C. Spend more time focusing on the positive qualities of his work.

    D. Look for another line of work that would make him more satisfied.

8. Leslie has recently married and moved to a new city. An appropriate way for Leslie to reduce her stress would be to:

    A. Try to change her old habits.

    B. Set aside some time each day to relax.

    C. Take a vacation with her husband.

    D. Take on extra work to keep her mind busy.

9. Sharon works on an assembly line where she watches metal fittings go by all day long. An appropriate way for Sharon to reduce her stress would be to:

    A. Bring in a soft cushion for her chair.

    B. Ask her boss if she can listen to a radio as she works.

    C. See if she can work through lunch so that she can finish her work as quickly as possible.

    D. Increase her workload to keep her mind occupied.

10. Karen has been planning on taking a week off from work. Now her boss tells Karen that it's impossible for her to have the vacation time she had planned. An appropriate way for Karen to reduce her stress would be to:
   A. Threaten to switch jobs unless she can take her vacation as planned.
   B. Act as if she didn't want the time off that much anyway.
   C. Tell her boss that she's disappointed and ask if she can take the time off next month.
   D. Act angry enough to convince her boss to give her the time off that she wanted.

11. Jennifer has four final exams and only two days left to study for them. An appropriate way for Jennifer to reduce her stress would be to:
   A. Take her mind off her own tests by helping a friend study.
   B. Pick the hardest course and study for that exam only.
   D. Study for each of her tests, one at a time.
   D. Try to spend twice as much time as she usually does studying for the exams.

12. Gwen wants to be president of a local club, but has been told that she lacks the organizational ability. An appropriate way for Gwen to reduce her stress would be to:
   A. Stop attending club meetings.
   B. Take a business class to improve her skills.
   C. Tell the club members that she doesn't really want to be the president.
   D. Accept the fact that she can never be the president.

13. Greg lives across from an all night gas station and is disturbed by the noise from the cars. An appropriate way for Greg to reduce his stress would be to:
   A. Play loud music to block out the noise.
   B. Take a sleeping pill to get to sleep.
   C. Give all of his business to another gas station.
   D. Use relaxation techniques to help block out noise.

14. Stanley is surrounded by people at a very crowded party. An appropriate way for Stanley to reduce his stress would be to:
   A. Stay in the middle of the crowd.
   B. Have several extra glasses of wine in order to relax.
   C. Loosen his tie so that he will feel more comfortable.

D. Get away from the crowd and stay in an area that's more comfortable for him.

15. Joyce must speak to a large group of people and keeps thinking about the time she was giving a speech in front of her class and forgot what she was going to say. An appropriate way for Joyce to reduce her stress would be to:
   A. Set aside some time before the speech to relax.
   B. Remember as many details as she can about her previous experience giving a speech.
   C. Keep her hands busy while she gives the speech.
   D. Review her speech until the last minute in order to be better prepared.

Scoring Key:
The responses to the preceding questions fall into one of five response categories. They are:

Appropriate   a response that is correct or appropriate for the situation.

Unhealthy   a response that is unhealthy.

Violation   a response that is in direct violation of the appropriate response to stress.

Denial   a response that denies the stress or the problem producing the stress.

Ineffective   a response that is related to the situation but is ineffective in reducing stress. It is neither unhealthy, nor in direct violation, nor a denial.

No.	Appropriate	Unhealthy	Violation	Denial	Ineffective
1.	C	—	A	D	B
2.	D	A	—	—	B, C
3.	C	A	B, D	—	—
4.	B	—	A	C	D
5.	A	C	C	—	B, D
6.	D	B	—	—	A, B
7.	C	—	—	—	A, D
8.	B	C	A, C	—	D
9.	B	—	D	—	A
10.	C	—	A, D	B	—
11.	C	—	A, D	—	B
12.	B	B	—	C	A, D
13.	D	B	A	—	C
14.	D	—	A	—	C
15.	A	—	B, D	—	C

STRESS SOURCE AND
RESISTANCE SURVEY

The following survey describes various conditions or times when people might feel stress. Read each statement and circle YES or NO to show if you would feel stress at that time. Each time you circle YES, place a number from 0 to 10 to show how certain you are that you could manage the stress from that situation. The 0 to 10 scale corresponds to the following certainty limits:

0	1	2	3	4	5	6	7	8	9	10
Very Uncertain				Somewhat Certain					Very Certain	

Situation	Might you feel stress?	If YES, how certain are you that you could manage the stress?
1. You're trying to concentrate, but you are constantly being interrupted.	YES/NO	_____
2. You have to do a very boring task.	YES/NO	_____
3. You've been thinking about someone who hurt you in the past.	YES/NO	_____
4. You have a neighbor who plays loud music all the time.	YES/NO	_____
5. You have several things to finish in a very short time.	YES/NO	_____
6. You're home by yourself and you feel lonely.	YES/NO	_____
7. You're in a crowded bus and can't get to the exit in time for your stop.	YES/NO	_____

8. You keep thinking about an   YES/NO   _____
   unpleasant experience.

9. You've taken on more than you   YES/NO   _____
   can do.

10. You're waiting on the street for   YES/NO   _____
    someone to pick you up and you're
    getting cold.

11. Although you have plenty of time,   YES/NO   _____
    you're worried you'll be late for an
    important appointment.

12. Your closest friend has left town   YES/NO   _____
    and you feel alone.

13. You're in a room that's extremely hot.   YES/NO   _____

14. You must buy a gift for someone   YES/NO   _____
    and stores are closing.

15. You saw someone being robbed   YES/NO   _____
    and keep imagining that it could
    happen to you.

16. You have to wait for a delivery and   YES/NO   _____
    you have nothing to do.

17. Your friends keep asking you to do   YES/NO   _____
    things you don't want to do.

18. You must get a prescription filled   YES/NO   _____
    and you can't find a drug store
    that's open.

19. You spend a good deal of time   YES/NO   _____
    in a place that's very noisy.

20. No matter how hard you've tried,   YES/NO   _____
    you haven't been able to finish
    all your work.

Scoring

1. Add all the numerical certainty scores _____
2. Count all the "YES" responses _____
3. Count all the "NO" responses _____
4. Divide No. 2 by No. 1 _____
5. Add No. 3 to No. 4 for a final score of _____

17-20 = Excellent stress resistance and management ability.
13-16 = Good stress resistance and good management ability.
10-12 = Fair stress resistance and management ability.
0-9   = Poor stress resistance and management ability.

This survey also can be used to indicate the number and types of stress situations in which you feel pressure. Count the number of "YES" responses. The maximum score of 20 indicates that you feel stress in all specified situations. The minimum score of 0 indicates that you feel stress in none of the specified situations.

In addition to an overall score, your responses also can be linked to specific stress sources. To determine the kinds of stresses you're susceptible to, compare the situations to which you responded YES and scored poorly on to the sources of stress below.

SOURCE OF STRESS	SITUATIONS			
Physical stress	4,	10,	13,	19
Frustration	1,	7,	14,	18
Emotional stress	3,	8,	11,	15
Poor time management	5,	9,	17,	20
Deprivation	2,	6,	12,	16

**STRESS MANAGEMENT
SURVEY**

This survey describes things that people might do to manage stress. Read each statement and circle YES or NO to show if you intend to do what's described in the item. Each time you circle YES, place a number from 0 to 10 to show how strong your intention is. The 0 to 10 scale corresponds to the following intention limits.

0	1	2	3	4	5	6	7	8	9	10
	Very								Very	
	Weak								Strong	

	Do you intend to do this?	If YES, how strong is your intention?
1. Find alternatives for goals you've been unable to reach.	YES/NO	_____
2. Stay away from crowded places if they make you feel nervous.	YES/NO	_____
3. Do the most important things first when you have too many things to do.	YES/NO	_____
4. Find interesting things to do when you're bored.	YES/NO	_____
5. Use earplugs when you're in noisy places.	YES/NO	_____
6. Avoid unnecessary changes when you have many other things to do.	YES/NO	_____
7. Look at the positive things in yourself and your life.	YES/NO	_____
8. Take one thing at a time.	YES/NO	_____

9. Get plenty of sleep every night.   YES/NO   _____

10. Talk about your problems with   YES/NO   _____
    friends and family.

11. Talk about your problems with the   YES/NO   _____
    people who are involved with them.

12. Balance work with relaxing activities.   YES/NO   _____

13. Use relaxation techniques.   YES/NO   _____

14. Get regular exercise.   YES/NO   _____

15. Avoid large amounts of caffeine.   YES/NO   _____

16. Try to identify what's causing   YES/NO   _____
    you stress.

17. Accept realistic goals for yourself   YES/NO   _____
    and others.

18. Avoid having many big changes   YES/NO   _____
    come at the same time.

19. Get professional help if you feel   YES/NO   _____
    too much stress.

20. Accept what you cannot change.   YES/NO   _____

Scoring
This survey can be scored in two ways, as follows:

A. Count the number of "YES" responses, disregarding the numerical
    intention scores. The maximum score of 20 means that you have
    a strong intention to use a variety of stress management tech-
    niques. A score of less than 15 indicates that you may or may not
    intend to utilize stress management in certain situations. You
    should evaluate the "NO" responses and determine why you can't.

B. Add all the numerical intention scores that correspond to the "YES" responses and divide the total number by 20 (the total number of items in the survey). The maximum score of 10 indicates a very strong intention to use stress management techniques. A score of 6 or less indicates that you have some work to do on specific areas of stress management and need to reevaluate how important it is for you to manage the stress in your life.

· Appendix ·

Health and Medical Resources

ASSOCIATIONS AND ORGANIZATIONS

Addiction and Recovery
Alcoholics Anonymous
P.O. Box 459, Grand Central Station, New York, NY 10163, (212) 870-3400
American Society of Addiction Medicine (ASAM)
4601 North Park Ave, Arcade Suite 101, Chevy Chase, MD 20815, (301)656-3920
Cocaine Anonymous
P.O. Box 2000, Los Angeles, CA 90049-8000, (310) 559-5833
International Drug Education Association (IDEA)
4213 Wiley Post Road, Dallas, TX, 75244, (972) 387-2230
National Association of Addiction Treatment Providers
501 Randolph Drive, Lititz, PA 17543-9049, (717) 581-1901
Sexaholics Anonymous
P.O. Box 111910, Nashville, TN 37222, (615) 331-6230
Society for the Study of Addiction
The National Addiction Centre, 4 Windsor Walk, London SE5 8AF, 44 (0)171 919 3841

Aging
Administration on Aging
330 Independence Avenue, SW, Washington, DC 20201, (800) 677-1116 or (202) 619-7501 (Aging Information Center)
Alzheimer's Association
919 N. Michigan Avenue, Suite 1000, Chicago, IL 60611-1676, (800) 272-3900

Alzheimer's Disease Education
P.O. Box 8250-JML, Silver Spring, MD 20907-8250, (301) 495-3311
Alzheimer's Foundation
8177 S. Harvard, M/C-114, Tulsa, OK 74137, (918) 743-0098
American Academy of Anti-Aging Medicine
2415 N. Greenview, Chicago, IL 60614, (773) 528-4333
American Society on Aging
833 Market Street, San Francisco, CA 94103, (415) 974-9600
Institute for Advanced Studies in Aging & Geriatric Medicine
1819 Pennsylvania Avenue, NW, Suite 400 Washington, DC 20006-3603, (202) 333-8845
National Council on Aging (NCOA)
409 Third Street, SW, Washington, DC 20024, (202) 479-1200
National Institute on Aging
Public Information Office, Building 31, Room 5C27, 31 Center Drive, MSC 2292, Bethesda, MD 20892, (301) 496-1752

AIDS/HIV
AIDS Education Global Information System (AEGIS)
P. O. Box 184, San Juan Capistrano, CA 92693-0184, (949) 248-5843
CDC Divisions of HIV/AIDS Prevention
1600 Clifton Rd., Atlanta, GA 30333, (404) 639-3311
International Association of Physicians in AIDS Care
33 North LaSalle Street, Chicago, IL 60602, (312) 795-4930
National AIDS Treatment Advocacy Project (NATAP)
580 Broadway, Suite 403, New York, NY 10012, (212) 219-0106
World Health Organization (WHO)
Avenue Appia 20, 1211 Geneva 27, Switzerland, (00 41 22) 791 21 11 or 525 23rd Street, NW, Washington, DC 20037, (202) 974-3000

Alternative Medicine
American Academy of Medical Acupuncture
5820 Wilshire Boulevard, Los Angeles, CA 90036, (323) 937-5514
American Alliance of Aromatherapy
P.O. Box 309, Depoe Bay, OR 97341, (800) 809-9850
American Holistic Health Association
P.O. Box 17400, Anaheim, CA 92817-7400, (714) 779-6152
American Massage Therapy Association
820 Davis St. Evanston, IL 60201, (847) 864-0123
American Music Therapy Association
8455 Colesville Road, Suite 1000, Silver Spring, MD 20910, (301) 589-3300
American Naturopathic Medical Association

P.O. Box 96273, Las Vegas, NV 89193, (702) 897-7053
American Society of Alternative Therapists
P.O. Box 703 Rockport, MA 01966, (978) 281-4400
Association for Applied Biofeedback
10200 W. 44th Avenue, Suite 304, Wheat Ridge, CO 80033-2840,
1-800-477-8892
National Center for Homeopathy
801 North Fairfax Street, Suite 306, Alexandria, VA 22314 (703)
548-7790

Cancer
American Cancer Society
1599 Clifton Road, N.E., Atlanta, GA 30329-4251, (404) 320-3333
American Institute for Cancer Research
1759 R Street, NW, Washington, DC 20069, 1-800-843-8114
Cancer Research Institute
133 East 58th Street, New York, NY 10022, (212) 688-7515
National Breast Cancer Foundation
18352 Dallas Parkway, Suite #136, Dallas, TX 75287,
Fax: (972) 248-6770
National Cancer Institute (NCI)
Bldg. 31, Rm. 10A03, 31 Center Drive, Bethesda, MD 20892-2580
(301) 435-3848

Health Associations
American Academy of Neurology
1080 Montreal Avenue, St. Paul, MN 55116, (651) 695-1940
American Diabetes Association
1660 Duke Street, Alexandria, VA 22314, (703) 232-3472
American Academy of Pain Management
13947 Mono Way #A, Sonora CA 95370, (209) 533-9744
American Chronic Pain Association
PO Box 850, Rocklin, CA 95677, (916) 632-0922
American College for Advancement in Medicine
23121 Verdugo Drive, Suite 204, Laguna Hills, CA 92653
American Heart Association
7320 Greenville Avenue, Dallas, TX 75231-4599, (214) 373-6300
American Public Health Association
800 I St., NW, Washington, DC 20001-3710, (202) 777-2742
Disabled Peoples' International
101-7 Evergreen Place, Winnipeg, Manitoba CANADA, R3L 2T3,
(204) 287-8010
International Pain Foundation

909 NE 43rd Street, Suite 306, Seattle WA 98105
National Vaccine Information Center
512 W. Maple Ave., Suite 206, Vienna, VA 22180, (703) 938-3783
Panic Disorder Institute
97 W. Bellevue Dr., Pasadena, CA 91105, (626) 577 8290
World Health Organization (WHO)
Avenue Appia 20, 1211 Geneva 27, Switzerland, (00 41 22) 791 21
11 or 525 23rd Street, NW, Washington, DC 20037, (202) 974-3000
World Oncology Network
1150 North 35th Avenue, Suite #170, Hollywood, FL 333021,(954)
986-6363

Nutrition/Eating Disorders
Academy for Eating Disorders
6728 Old McLean Village Drive, McLean, VA 22101-3906, (703) 556-
9222
American College of Nutrition
301 E 17th St.New York, NY 10003, (212) 777-1037
The American Society for Clinical Nutrition
9650 Rockville Pike, Bethesda, MD 20814-3998, (301)530-7110
American Dietetic Association
216 W. Jackson Blvd., Chicago, IL 60606-6995, (312) 899-0040
Council for Responsible Nutrition
1875 Eye Street, NW, Suite 400, Washington, DC 20006-5409, (202)
872-1488
Institute of Human Nutrition
630 West 168th St., Presbyterian Hospital 15 East, New York, NY
10032
Linus Pauling Institute
Oregon State University, 571 Weniger Hall, Corvallis, Oregon 97331,
(541) 737-5075

Psychological/Mental Health
Anxiety Disorders Association of America
11900 Parklawn Drive, Suite 100, Rockville, MD 20852,
(301) 231-9350
Depression and Affective Disorders Association
Johns Hopkins Hospital, 600 N. Wolfe Street, Meyer 3-181,
Baltimore, MD 21205, (410) 955-4647
National Alliance on Schizophrenia and Depression
60 Cutter Mill Road, Great Neck, NY 11021, (516) 829-0091
National Institute for the Psychotherapies

330 West 58th Street, New York, NY 10019, (212) 582-1566
National Institute of Mental Health (NIMH)
6001 Executive Boulevard, Rm. 8184, MSC 9663, Bethesda, MD
20892-9663, (301) 443-4513
Obsessive-Compulsive Foundation
P.O. Box 70, Milford, CT 06460-0070, (203) 878-5669

Reproduction/Sex Issues
American Social Health Association (ASHA)
PO Box 13827, Research Triangle Park, NC 27709, (919) 361-8400
Family Health International (FHI)
P.O. Box 13950, Research Triangle Park, NC 27709, (919) 544-7040
Family Health International HIV/AIDS Department
2101 Wilson Boulevard, Suite 700, Arlington, VA 22201,
(703) 516-9779
Fertility Foundation
P.O. Box 18627, Charlotte, NC 28205, (704) 531-8345
Impotence Institute of America
119 S. Ruth Street. Maryville, TN 37801, (800) 669-1603
In Vitro International
16632 Millikan Avenue, Irvine, CA 92606, (800) 246-8487
Male Sexual Dysfunction Clinic
4940 Eastern Avenue, Baltimore, MD 21224, (410) 550-2329
National Women's Health Network
1325 G Street, NW, Washington, DC 20005, (202) 347-1140
Office of Population Affairs
4350 East West Highway, Suite 200 West, Bethesda, MD 20814,
(301) 594-4000

Stress and Stress Management
American Academy of Experts in Traumatic Stress
368 Veterans Memorial Highway, Commack, NY 11725,
(516) 543-2217
American Institute of Stress
124 Park Ave., Yonkers, NY 10703, (914) 963-1200
International Society for Traumatic Stress Studies
60 Revere Drive, Suite #500, Northbrook, IL 60062, (847) 480-9028
International Stress Management Association
Division of Psychology, South Bank University, 103 Borough Road,
London SE1 0AA, 07000 780430

GOVERNMENT HEALTH AND MEDICAL INFORMATION AGENCIES

Centers for Disease Control and Prevention (CDC)
1600 Clifton Rd., Atlanta, GA 30333, (404) 639-3311
Department of Health and Human Services (DHHS)
200 Independence Avenue, SW, Washington, DC 20201, (202) 619-0257
Department of Veteran Affairs
810 Vermont Avenue, NW, Washington, DC 20420, (202) 273-5771
Food and Consumer Service – USDA
14th & Independence Ave. SW, Washington, DC 20250, (202) 720-2791
Food and Drug Administration (FDA)
5600 Fishers Lane, Rockville, MD 20857, (888) 463-6332
Food Safety and Inspection Service
Room 2932-South Building; 1400 Independence Ave. SW, Washington, DC 20250, (202) 720-7943
National Cancer Institute (NCI)
Bldg. 31, Rm. 10A03, 31 Center Drive, Bethesda, MD 20892-2580, (301) 435-3848
National Center for Biotechnology Information (NCBI)
Building 38A, Room 8N805, Bethesda, MD 20894, (301) 496-2475
National Health Information Center (NHIC)
P.O. Box 1133, Washington, DC 20013-1133, (301) 565-4167
National Heart, Lung, and Blood Institute Information Center
PO Box 30105, Bethesda, MD 20824-0105, (301) 951-3260
National Institutes of Health (NIH)
Bethesda, MD 20892
National Institute of Mental Health (NIMH)
6001 Executive Boulevard, Rm. 8184, MSC 9663, Bethesda, MD 20892-9663, (301) 443-4513
National Institute of Neurological Disorders and Stroke
P.O. Box 5801 Bethesda, MD 20824
National Institute on Aging
Public Information Office. Building 31, Room 5C27, 31 Center Drive, MSC 2292, Bethesda, MD 20892, (301) 496-1752
National Institute on Drug Abuse
6001 Executive Blvd., Bethesda, MD, 20892-9561, (301) 443-1124
National Library of Medicine
8600 Rockville Pike, Bethesda, MD 20894, (888) 346-3656
National Science Foundation

4201 Wilson Boulevard, Arlington, VA 22230, (703) 306-1234
Occupational Safety and Health Administration (OSHA)
Office of Public Affairs - Room N3647, 200 Constitution Avenue,
Washington, DC 20210, (202) 693-1999

HEALTH & MEDICAL WEB SITES

Consumer Health Information
Achoo: *http://www.achoo.com*
AIDS & HIV Information Resource: *http://www.thebody.com*
AMA Health Insight: *http://ama-assn.org/consumer.htm*
Dr. Koop: *http://www.drkoop.com*
Drug Information Database: *http://www.infodrug.com*
Health A to Z: *http://www.healthatoz.com*
Health News Network: *http://www.healthnewsnet.com*
Heart and Stroke A to Z Guide: *http://www.americanheart.org*
HIV Daily Briefing (updated hourly): *http://www.aegis.com*
Infectious Diseases Society: *http://www.idsociety.org*
Mayo Clinic Health Oasis: *http://www.mayohealth.org*
MD Advice: *http://www.mdadvice.com*
Medicine Net: *http://www.medicinenet.com*
Medicine Online: *http://www.meds.com*
Mediconsult: *http://www.mediconsult.com*
Medscape: *http://www.medscape.com*
National Institute of Stress Physiology: *http//www.nisp.org*
National Woman's Health Resource Center (NWHRC):
http://www.healthywoman.org
On Health: *http://www.onhealth.com*
RxList (internet drug index): *http://www.rxlist.com*
Women's Healthnet: *http://intl.womenshealthnet.com*
World Health Statistics (WHOSIS): *http://www.who.int/whosis/*

Government Health Information Resources
Cancer Net: *http://cancernet.nci.nih.gov*
CDC AIDS/HIV Clearinghouse: *http://www.cdcnpin.org*
CDC Diabetes Home Page: *http://www.cdc.gov/diabetes*
Centers for Disease Control (CDC): *http://www.cdc.gov*
Federal Statistics (FedStats): *http://www.fedstats.gov*
Food, Nutrition and Consumer Services: *http://www.fns.usda.gov*
Healthfinder: *http://www.healthfinder.gov/news*
Health Resources and Services Administration (HRSA):
http://www.hrsa.dhhs.gov/newsroom

National Cancer Institute (NCI): *http://www.nci.nih.gov*
National Center for Health Statistics: *http://www.cdc.gov/nch-swww*
Nutrient Data Laboratory: *http://www.nal.usda.gov/fnic/foodcomp*
National Eye Institute: *http://www.nei.nih.gov*
National Institute of Allergy and Infectious Diseases (NIAID): *http://www.niaid.nih.gov*
National Institute of Arthritis and Musculoskeletal and Skin Diseases (NIAMS): *http://www.nih.gov/niams*
National Institute of Child Health and Human Development: *http://www.nichd.nih.gov*
National Institute of Diabetes and Digestive and Kidney Diseases: *http://www.niddk.nih.gov*
National Institute of General Health Sciences (NIGHS): *http://www.nih.gov/nighs*
National Institute of Environmental Health Sciences (NIEHS): *http://www.niehs.nih.gov*
National Institutes of Health (NIH): *http://www.nih.gov*
National Institutes of Mental Health: *http://www.nimh.nih.gov*
National Institute of Neurological Disorders and Stroke: *http://www.ninds.nih.gov*
National Institute on Alcohol Abuse and Alcoholism (NIAAA): *http://www.niaaa.nih.gov*
National Institute on Deafness and Other Communicative Disorders (NIDCD): *http://www.nih.gov/nidcd*
National Institute on Drug Abuse (NIDA): *http://www.nida.nih.gov*
Office of Human Radiation Experiments: *http://tis.eh.doe.gov/ohre*
Office of Minority Health Resource Center: *http://www.omhrc.gov*
Public Health Service: *http://phs.os.dhhs.gov/phs*
Substance Abuse and Mental Health Services Administration: *http://www.samhsa.gov*
U.S. Department of Health and Human Services (DHHS): *http://www.os.dhhs.gov*
U.S. Department of Veteran Affairs: *http://www.va.gov*
U.S. Food and Drug Administration (FDA): *http://www.fda.gov*
U.S. Vital Health Facts and Statistics: *http://www.cdc.gov/nch-swww/fastats/fastats.htm*